Surviving Yellowstone:
A Holiday Turned Deadly

Artistic Rendering of McCarthy's Mammoth Springs Hotel

By
William E. Cecrle

For my wife, who allows me to research and write

To Dad and Mom, who instilled a love of the Wyoming wilderness

"I know one that did not close his eyes, and that was your humble servant. I felt as though someone ought to stay awake; if the truth was known, I felt pretty nervous."

        Andrew Weikert, Helena Party

Approaching the place where the Alum Creek disgorged itself into the churning waters to join the flow to Yellowstone Lake they knew that they were nearing camp. They turned their horses up the creek and passed through a stand of timber. Coming into a glade that descended into a small oval meadow, Andy let his horse have its head. Wilkie was a few rods behind him on the trail and Andy was beginning to turn and talk when from the corner of his eye he saw the heads of Indians bobbing up from behind a fallen tree at the base of the hill. He had rode within a mere 75 yards of the log; it was an ambush!

His eyes widened with fear and he yelled, "Indians!" He attempted to wheel his horse around and simultaneously readied his rifle. Looking back at the log he saw no less than a half dozen rifles leveled at him. He played "Injun" and made himself as small as he could, with his gun across his knees. His horse continued to fight his efforts to turn around; it knew they were headed back to camp and did not understand why he suddenly wanted to change course. A series of rifle reports and bullets zipping past sent his horse hopping in surprise and panic. No projectiles struck him but he was at risk for losing any control of his horse.

Andy yanked his reigns to turn his horse after Wilkie. He saw a half-dozen more rifles heading to shoulders as he finally wrest control of his horse and spun it around. He spurred his horse mercilessly in the ribs to follow Wilkie, who had been able to turn around at his first shout.

A cluster of gunfire erupted behind him. In the same moment, Andy felt the unmistakable punch of a bullet as it sliced a four-inch long cut along and tore a chip out of his shoulder blade. It knocked him forward against his saddle horn but he maintained his seat in the saddle. Now in full gallop, his horse leapt a dry seasonal creek bed. As it gained the other side another barrage of fire erupted and again Andy felt the slap of a bullet; this time it had ripped a chunk from the stock of his rifle. He hugged even closer to his horse's neck but there was no more room to flatten himself.

Other Works in Surviving Yellowstone

T.C. Everts' 37 Days of Peril

The Last Great American Indian War Part I

The Last Great American Indian War Part II

The Last Great American Indian War Part III

The Radersburg Revenant

Copyright © 2019 by Cyclopean Phoenix & William E. Cecrle Publishing Co.
All rights reserved.
Printed in the United States of America

Published by Kindle Direct Publishing

Legend

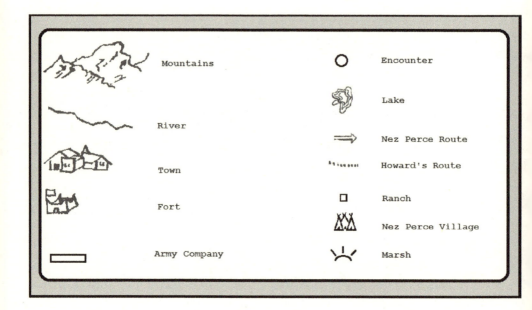

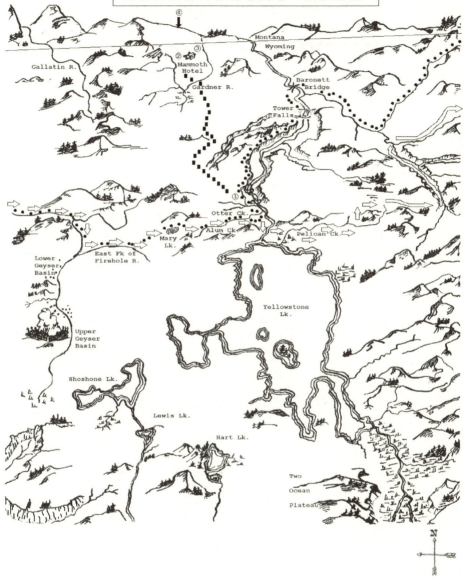

Surviving Yellowstone:
A Holiday Turned Deadly

By
William E. Cecrle

1. Joe. Roberts. 2. Andrew Weikert. 3. Fred. Pfister. 4. Chas. Kence. 5. Prof. Richard Deitrich. 6. Leonard Duncan. 7. Ben. Stone.

Table of Contents

Preface 13
Prelude 15
Battle of Big Hole 15
Yellowstone Park 35
    The Helena Party 39
Appendix 121
Helena Party Accounts 121
Works Consulted 135
End Notes 138

Preface

The Helena Party's encounter with the Nez Perce, was an event that took place during the Nez Perce War of 1877. This war has been widely documented. As it has been noted elsewhere, the winners get to write the history; but this is a rare case. The "losing side", in this narrative the Nez Perce, also contributed significantly to the historical account.

Those Nez Perce who escaped to Canada were later interviewed by reporters and authors wanting the Indians' perspective. Free from fear of reprisal or pressure to conform, the survivors were able to give what they experienced and how they understood those events.

The accounts of the "winning side" were recorded in letters and books published by those involved, military and court documents, newspaper articles, and government monuments to the campaign. Many of these sources were testimonies immediately taken after the events and others recollections of the survivors years or decades later.

This book is a history book, but not of the same sterile name-date-event textbooks that we all were subjected to in our secondary educations. This book uses narrative history as the *modus operandi* to relay the information to the reader. It maintains a traditional narrative focus on events, their chronology, the places, and the people and their actions. The author sincerely hopes that the readers find the story as unbiased and fair as can be expected with the temporal distance from the events.

Prelude

August 9th

Battle of Big Hole

Big Hole River, Montana Territory

The men silently picked their way through the alternating pine groves and marshlands. They navigated by the starlight but the dimness was far from ideal; they would trip over fallen timber and stub toes against rocks jutting from the trail. In the marshy areas they could not see the dry clumps of vegetation or ground to step on; soon all their boots softly squished with brackish mud-water. Sections of the column would get lost, requiring the remainder of the column to hold up and wait for them.

Finally the column achieved the foothills just before the valley floor. They hugged to the hillside and travelled on the left fork of the trail. Soon they came within view of the distant village where teepees glowed in the night from their lodge fires and a few of the bonfires' coals radiated orange-red light. Occasionally the baying of a dog pierced the night.

The vanguard was now on the hillside directly above and across the river from the village. As they stealthily exited a strip of timber extending down into the valley, they came face to face with a grazing horse herd. The horses stopped clipping grass and lifted their heads to look at the column of men. Then they commenced neighing. The men silently cursed them and moved as quickly past as stealth could afford. The horses did not become alarmed, running off and alerting the Indians below. The men still had the advantage of surprise!

They had made it close enough now to discern the outlines of the teepees in the bottom below and Gibbon ordered a halt by way of chain of whispers. Everyone lay down within earshot of the barking dogs, crying babies, and other noises of the camp. They were at best 30 yards above the dense blanket of willows lining the banks of the river where the village slept. Gibbon retrieved his pocket watch from his vest and angled it in the starlight; it showed 2 AM. The mountain, hills, and valley were still: but of the quiet that preceded a tornado.

Gibbon considered the importance of capturing the horse herd they had passed through. The original plan had been to stampede them so that his main force could arrive and engage the Indians. Now that his main force was in position he decided against molesting the horses since it might wake their guards. The officers were told via hand signals to converge on Gibbon, now a mere 400 feet from the village. The 89 lodges had been erected in a straggling open V running northeast to southwest on the valley side of the river. Now having seen the topography and how the camp was situated, they could make an informed plan of attack.

Gibbon made certain the leaders all had their watches. They took them out and synchronized their times. "We will attack at *exactly* four o'clock, just before dawn." He said looking each man in the eyes to push home his point.

Volunteer Captain Catlin was assigned to lead the volunteers in accompaniment of Lieutenant Bradley's K Company. They would cross the swampy marsh on the extreme left of the village. Captains Richard Comba and James Sanno were to arrange the men of D Company as skirmishers and cross the stream at the front of the village. Volunteer Captains Rawn and Constant Williams would remain in the current position in support roles. Captain Logan would lead A Company in from the extreme right of the village.

"Make certain the men aim low in the teepees. We will give three volleys, then charge the village." He ordered as the meeting concluded.

The officers scuttled back to their men and disseminated the orders. Within minutes all the companies were on the move, heading to their ordered fighting positions; their furtive movements imperceptible to the sleeping villagers. By 4 AM all had successfully reached their positions without alerting the Indians.

Just before dawn they launched the attack on the sleeping camp. Everyone pushed forward in perfect silence and scarcely a sound issued from the camp itself. The men, anticipating the fight, all began to advance quicker. Bradley and Sanno pushed through the underbrush and into the mucky slough. At that very moment, Comba's company worked their way across a 30-foot boggy peninsula in the winding stream. After crossing the brown-water bog, they approached the willow thickets lining the west bank opposite of the village. These were so thick that their skirmish line was broken into smaller segments as men funneled into the only openings available.

The volunteers with Captain Catlin were almost to the river when a lone Indian came riding towards them on a large iron-gray horse. They pushed themselves into the surrounding cover. The Indian was a large, well-built fellow but his business seemed to occupy his attention. The trajectory of his path was to the herd of horses the soldiers had passed earlier. It was not until he was within a few yards of the men that he noticed them.

Instantly he heeled his horse in an attempt to ride through the line of soldiers. Four shots range out in unison and the force of the bullets ripped the man from his horse's back. The shots echoed through the valley as the horse galloped away at full speed.

Chief White Bird was also on his way to tend his horses. He was on foot, however, and about 40 steps behind *Wetistokaith*, a member of Joseph's band. The man was severely near sighted and could not see the soldiers until it was too late. White Bird wheeled around yelling, "We are attacked! We are attacked!"

Captain Comba led D Company on a rapid advance when the first shots ripped through the morning silence. Rushing to within 75 feet of the riverbank, Comba order them to fire and they delivered a volley low into the teepees.

Five-year-old Red Wolf was in his teepee sleeping when the first volley ripped through the home. His two brothers leapt up and ran for cover in the willows. His mother gathered up his little sister and, taking him by the hand, they started to run after his brothers.

A single shot passed through her and the baby. She dropped down without saying a word. His father bent over her and checked each body. Although Red Wolf did not realize it, both were dead. Bullets were flying past everywhere. His father tried to take his hand and pull the dazed boy with him, but the child would not leave his mother. Seeing that he was determined to stay there, the father covered him with the family's big buffalo robe and ordered him to stay perfectly still. Then his father dashed into the willows.

Red Wolf was alone and frightened as the sound of guns and the screaming wounded increased. But he never moved. He tried not to cry, "I must be brave," he told himself as he choked back the tears.[i]

Seeing the stream was fordable in front of them, Comba gave the order to charge. He did not want to be caught on the wrong side of the water. The men promptly obeyed and within moments were in the enemy village. They shouted a loud battle cry that rivaled the Indians and engaged the enemies.

At the very moment that Comba had delivered his volleys into the teepees, Bradley with K Company and the volunteers had attacked the village from the left side. They shouted and fired a volley into those teepees. Sleeping in their teepee, *Wetyetmas Likleinen* (Circling Swan) and his wife died in this volley. Blindly shot bullets also claimed the life of *Tewit Toitoi* asleep in the adjacent lodge. There was almost no resistance initially. Half-naked men and women were diving into brush and any other cover they could find.

Then Bradley, who knew no fear, gave the order to charge the village. As he entered a thicket where braves had been seen one of his company shouted, "Hold on, Lieutenant; don't go in there; it's sure death!"

Bradley pushed ahead anyways. Captain Catlin was struggling through the last of the willows beside the lieutenant when a bullet zipped past and stuck the former in the head, killing him instantly. Shouting for the men to push forward Catlin then saw one of his volunteers, David Morrow, take bullet and fall dead to the ground. While rushing past him Catlin saw Morrow's hat with a bullet hole through the crown, plainly telling the cause of his death.

Private Hurlburt had a vantage point to see Bradley's death through a long opening in the willows. Moreover, he had a similar open corridor where he saw the Indian who pulled the trigger. Rushing forward with the line he kept his eyes on the man. As they were braking through the last of the willows, he pulled the butt of his rifle tight into his shoulder. Still focused on the same Indian he aimed at the Indian's chest. Squeezing the trigger the rifle bucked against his shoulder and the warrior folded over. He had killed him, avenging his officer's death.

From the edge of the willows, Yellow Wolf watched as First Sergeant Frederick Stortz stood paralyzed, rigid as though he was dead or a statue. As the Indian shouldered his rifle he noted the strips on the shoulder of the man's uniform. Stortz stood without moving and was staring at him. Even as Yellow Wolf took aim and fired, the man's only movement was the widening of his eyes as he witnessed his own death. The shot killed him instantly.

Yellow Wolf raced into the battle. He ran past the teepee of a very old man, *Wahnistas Aswetesk.* There sat the old man upon a buffalo robe smoking. He had been shot many times, blood oozing and trickling from various points of his body. As Yellow Wolf watched, a soldier ran past, stopped, and then shot the old man. Still he sat there. Others shot him. He did not move, just sat there smoking as if only raindrops struck him! It looked to Yellow Wolf as though 20 bullets had entered his body. The old man did not feel the shots![ii]

Shore Crossing had been pulling on his moccasins and his wife stoking the fire when the gunfire rang out. They shared a quick, knowing look. Grabbing his rifle, Shore Crossing jumped through the teepee flap and entered the fray.

Jumping into a shallow depression near their teepee, he laid flat and propped his rifle across a thigh-thick log. He shouldered his rifle and began firing at the appearing soldiers. Moments later his wife was by his side. The depression did not offer one person, let alone two, good cover.

He looked to his left and saw *Wahchumyus* (Rainbow), another powerful warrior. He was four steps away, also shooting into the willow thicket. Rainbow was known to be fearless in battle. He had the special protection of his *wyakin* (guardian spirit), who had told him that he could not die in any battle fought after sunrise. This afforded the young man unnatural courage that won the respect of his fellow Nez Perce.

Shore Crossing yelled to his wife, "Go with people to hiding!"

She leaped up to go as instructed. But as she started to go a bullet hit her with a loud slap and spun her around. She lay on the ground a few feet from her husband and yelled to him that she was shot.

The battle raged around him. He turned and yelled to the warriors around him, "My wife is shot to die! I will not leave her! I will go nowhere! I am staying here until killed!"

At the moment he turned back towards the willows a soldier burst through and Shore Crossing dropped him with a single shot. Another soldier, seeing the flash of the rifle took aim and shot him through the head. He flipped onto his back, limbs flailing and twitching. The primary instigator of the war had perished in its blazing fury.[iii]

Rainbow saw his friend die; their determined resistance had failed. He leapt to his feet and fled to the nearby brush. Bullets whizzed past him as he ran, but none seemed to have found its mark.

Shore Crossing's wife ignored her severe injuries and rolled to the shallow depression. There she grabbed her husband's loaded rifle; the one belonging to Richard Devine that had fired the initial bullet of the present war. The soldier who had killed Shore Crossing moved forward into the open. She took aim, shot, and killed him. Then a pair of soldiers quickly aimed at her and pulled their triggers. She rose up in a death throe, and as she bled out she lay across her husband's chest as if protecting him.

The advance of Company K had been momentarily halted by their pocket of resistance. It had bought the time for other Indians to arm themselves and put up a more robust defense.

At this time, Captain Sanno had made it through the willows and across the river. They had emerged at the point of the "V" Gibbon assumed the village's shape to be. 180 feet from the edge of the village they delivered their first volley, with several men concentrating fire on a lone teepee slightly set apart from the rest. They had noticed a high level of activity at it while they waited for the 4 o'clock hour to strike. Certain it was full of gambling braves they had dedicated a few men to pour lead into it, ensuring the braves did not come out fighting. They reloaded and let go with their second volley. Knowing their role, everyone rushed forward into the village without needing the order.

They ripped open the first teepee to discover it was a maternity lodge, not a gambler's lodge. A squaw, *Weyatanatoo*

Latpat's wife, had just delivered a baby. The squaw was dead and next to her was another dead elderly squaw, *Tissaikpee,* her nurse. The newborn lay screaming, still wrapped in the mother's arms. A soldier stepped forward and smashed in its head with the butt of his rifle and moved to the next teepee.

He entered the teepee and was confronted by a barking and growling dog. He put a quick bullet through its chest and left to continue his rampaging. In his haste, he neglected to notice the bulging mass of blankets in the corner of the teepee. Under the blankets lay three boys; young *Pahit Palikt*, his older 12-year-old brother, and a 13-year-old cousin. The brothers' mother and father had covered them telling them to stay hidden; being low they would not be hit by bullets. Then the parents ran from the teepee.

After the soldier had left, his brother shook his shoulder saying, "Wake up! Bring that blanket and come!"

He grabbed his blanket and they all three ran with all their might from the teepee. Guns were firing fast and loud! They had run maybe 30 steps when his brother leapt over the creek bank and called to him, "Jump down here!"

Pahit Palikt jumped to him and they hid in the brush. For maybe half an hour, or perhaps a full one; the boy could not tell, the soldiers seemed to be shooting at them. He heard bullets whizzing and whining overhead the entire time.

Finally his brother was hit by one of the bullets. He died next to him under the bank. The young boy missed his blanket. He thought, "*Where is my blanket?*"

Then he remembered dropping it while running for the creek's bank. He peeked his head up and saw no soldiers around; they had all passed by. He jumped up and raced over to the blanket. In a single swift move he grabbed it and spun back towards the bank. Moments later he returned to the relative safety of the creek bank.

A bullet from one of his own men had grazed Sanno's head but there was no time to stop. They continued rushing through the village and were met by a group of knife-wielding young boys. Intending to protect their families, they attempted to stop the soldiers with the hand-held weapons. Sanno swung the butt of his rifle to knock the children out of the way and continued forward. His men followed suit, disabling the children with crippling blows of rifle stocks and barrels.

Chief White Bird's ten-year-old son, also named White Bird, was still in their teepee with his siblings. Bullets came like hail on the skin walls and the poles. They decided to make a run for it and raced for the stream. At its bank they dove into the water without hesitation, both were wounded. Three others had joined them. Then shortly after two girls arrived. One had been shot through the upper arm; she dunked it in the ice-cold water to numb it. When she lifted it out, the wound was so big White Bird could see through the bullet hole.

Suhm Keen (Shirt On) was sleeping beside his grandmother *Chee-Nah* (Martha Joseph) when the shooting started. The grandmother stood to peer out the teepee flap when a bullet pierced her shoulder. Blood streaming from the wound, she pushed him from the teepee crying, "Shirt On, run to the trees and hide!" Obeying without question, he ran toward a low ridge at the mouth of a gulch while bullets kept whizzing past clipping off leaves and branches all around him.

He made it to the brush and hid himself. He was very afraid. Soon some other boys had also escaped to the ridge. They joined him there and watched trembling as the awful sight below unfold.

By this time, Indian marksmen had made their way up the surrounding slopes. They took up positions on the eastern bluff and began firing down at the soldiers. The snipers were doling out considerable damage to the attackers. Seeing the Montana volunteers increased their fury. They had lived up to their side of the Lolo Canyon treaty! They had left the settlers of the Bitterroot in peace! Another betrayal by the white man! They were never to be trusted!

Company A under Captain Logan entered the extreme right of the maelstrom on the run. They emerged directly behind Indians sheltering behind the banks of the stream. The soldiers leveled their guns at the unarmed men, women, and children and began killing them.

An order was given to expose those hiding in lodges. Some soldiers tore at the hide walls, slashing them with their knives. Others employed ropes to pull over the structures while their fellow soldiers waited to dispatch any occupants.

A sergeant moving through the teepees saw a squaw with the vacant stare of the dead. Her infant lay astride her corpse screaming and flailing an arm shattered by a bullet. He continued past and saw robes and blankets floating down the stream. One soldier shouted and they all turned to see an Indian jumping into the stream beneath a blanket, trying to escape the carnage.

The men quickly aimed and fired at all the robes, blankets, and other debris in the stream. Anything that could conceal a person was shot. Soon bodies were floating up out from beneath the covers. The bodies and hiding material all slowly disappeared around the bend in the stream.

In less than 20 minutes the soldiers had complete control of that section of village and commenced destroying it. They set fire to the teepees but some were too damp from the morning dew to do more than smolder. The camp, already filled with black powder smoke from their weapons, now was enveloped in the smoke of burning hides and lodge poles.

Seeing the burning homes *Kowtoliks*, a brave warrior, cried in a loud voice, "My brothers! Our teepees are on fire! Get ready your arms! Make resistance! You are here for that purpose!" he rallied a small group of men. They tried to push back the soldiers to extinguish the flames. But, they were too few and their attack was repelled.

From one of the teepees the cries of children who had been hiding beneath buffalo robes escalated into shrieks of pain as the flames enveloped them. Soon the teepee produced no sound but crackling of fire as the flames licked at the lodge poles. These soon gave way, collapsing the teepee on itself. The soldiers scattered the food and supplies lying around the homes.

Gibbon had the advantage of surprise but had squandered it. He and his men soon were on the defensive. At one end of the village White Bird rallied the warriors hiding in the willows. The old warrior bellowed in their native tongue,

> Why are we retreating? Since the world was made brave men fight for their women and children. Are we going to run to the mountains and let the whites kill our women

and children before our eyes? It is better
we should be killed fighting. Now is our
time to fight! These soldiers cannot fight
harder than the ones we defeated in White
Bird Canyon. Fight! Shoot them down. We can
shoot as well as any of these soldiers!

This speech stemmed the retreat. The warriors faced and conquered their fear. Then they turned around with purpose. They dodged back through the battle and into their homes. There they retrieved their weapons and went to fight the soldiers.

At the other side of the camp, Looking Glass was attempting the same feat. Not knowing Shore Crossing had already died he called out,

Waalize! Tap-sic-ill-pilp! Um-til-lilp-
Crown! This is a battle! These men are not
asleep as those you murdered in Idaho! These
soldiers mean battle! You tried to break my
promise at Lolo, you wanted to fight at the
fortified place. Now it is time to show your
courage and fight. You can kill right and
left. I would rather see you killed than the

rest of the warriors, for you commenced the war. Now go ahead and fight.

The fighting continued in small pockets at the south end of the village where the initial attack had occurred. These firefights were scattered and small. Many of the soldiers and Indians lost their lives in those moments, carpeting the village floor with blood and bodies. But the soldiers continued to drive the villagers back.

Within an hour's time the army had overrun the majority of the village. But now they were spread out and Indian sharpshooters were on all the surrounding hillsides pinning men down, occasionally picking one off. Squaws had been picking up the weapons of their dead husbands, brothers, and fathers and killing soldiers with as much skill and courage as the men.

Colonel Gibbon rode down the old Indian trail from where he had observed the attack. He crossed the river and approached his men who were pulling down and vainly attempting to torch teepees. He dismounted and was taking in the scene around him when an officer nearby yelled at him that his horse had been shot.

Gibbon glanced back and was shocked to see the poor beast had his foreleg broken near the knee. He then recalled having felt a slight slap on his leg while crossing the water. It took him a moment to discover that the same bullet that broke his horse's leg had passed through his own; but he was more fortunate in the fact that it had not broken his bone. His mind spun and in shock he hobbled back a few steps and plunged into the cold water, allowing it to stream over his boot tops.

The cold of the water recalled him to his senses. One of the sharpshooters on the eastern bluff or the slope of the mountain to the west must have shot him! Looking around more alertly, the Colonel realized that their position had become untenable. There were also Indian sharpshooters in the willows lining the river. His men were surrounded by hostiles lurking in and around the smoldering village and occupying the high ground on 2 sides. Even worse, their element of surprise had worn off and the villagers had begun to collect and organize themselves.

Remaining where they were would only increase casualties and decrease their ability to retaliate. He ordered a retreat back up the bluffs they had left earlier, and in the direction of the point of timber jutting down into the valley.

The men slowly assembled because it was difficult and slow to get word to all. Then they made ready for withdrawal, demoralizing as it was. The guns of fallen comrades were broken or flung into the river, they searched for and attended to the wounded, and missing men were searched for.

The group made ready for retreat. When the order was given, off they went through the gauntlet. They made a mad dash across an open glade in the valley; running as fast as their bodies would go and fear could drive them. Several soldiers were cut down by more snipers' bullets in the crossing.

Pointing out the best defensive position, a lopsided vase-shaped depression 200 feet long, he ordered the men to take it. They rushed up the hill to it, driving the Indians sniping from it further back up the hillside. Orders were shouted to dig in. Men pulled out knives, bayonets, cups, tin plates, and anything else at hand with which to dig.

Soldiers provided covering fire while others fortified their position. Downed trees and stumps were placed along the perimeter and holes between the timbers were filled with rock and dirt. The latter becoming readily available as the men continued to burrow rifle pits.

The men heard the Indians as they returned to the village below. Individual cries pierced the air as squaws found dead husbands, sons, and brothers and braves found dead wives, mothers, daughters, and sisters. Soon the village was full of cries mixing into a cacophony. Not a man on the hill would ever forget the wail of mingled grief, rage, and horror that arose from the camp.[iv]

Late in the afternoon the soldiers watched as the industrious Indians dismantled the entire village and packed it up. Soon a column of horses, squaws, old men and chiefs started south. The warriors conspicuously stayed behind but out of rifle range.

August 10th

Big Hole River, Montana Territory

Finally the wait was over. The sun crested the eastern horizon spilling warmth and light across the valley floor and into the soldiers' crude fortification. The Nez Perce shooting had substantially declined by this point. The warriors had begun slowly withdrawing to catch up with their families. Though no Nez Perce family had been untouched by the village massacre, some men felt its sting more sharply than others. These men volunteered to remain behind longer, the desire for revenge burned brighter in them and they would not pass up an opportunity to kill more soldiers.

They saw what appeared to be the last of the warriors disappearing down the trail. No shots having been heard for hours, the colonel ordered the men into skirmish lines and they returned to the battle site. When all the men had been accounted for, they were buried.

Yellowstone Park

August 25th

Hayden Valley

James Irwin stood up with his bedding and strapped it onto the back of his saddle. He was a well-built young man in his mid twenties and had the efficient movements and mannerisms of a soldier, which he should considering he had just completed an army service commitment. On July 17 he had received a surgeon's certificate of disability and been honorably discharged from Fort Ellis.

Jim, as he was called, had figured that being young and single it was an ideal time to tour the new Yellowstone National Park. He surmised that he might never be back to this area in his lifetime. Even if he did he would likely be married or at the very least older and less capable of wilderness exploration.

So, he had set off for a solo trip into the wilderness. That was just over a month past and he had covered much of the park in that time and seen what he believed to be most of its wonders. He had seen almost no one else during his tour and anyone he met had been leisurely.

But, the past day had a different feel to it. He had seen ten men riding by Sulphur Mountain. He had taken out his telescope to observe who they were. They had been in various states of speed, some in full-blown running and others in gallops. They appeared to be in a hurry but he could not see any cause. Because of the time of day he guessed they were in a hurry to set up camp. He knew of a couple good spots on the path they traveled. He had spent some time there when he had first arrived in the park. Perhaps today he would go see them?

He straightened his cavalry coat, stepped into a stirrup, and swung onto the saddle. Suddenly a band of Indians crested the ridge a short distance away. Turning in his saddle, he saw as another group appeared to his other side. His heart leapt in his throat and he quickly dismounted. Peering over the saddle he swore as the Indians heeled their ponies his way. He knew they had seen him and there was no hope for escape.

The farther group saw him first and with a series of war whoops headed his direction. The closer group then noticed him and descended upon him too. Irwin knew that his wits alone could save him, fighting was useless.

As the leader came close Irwin put up a hand, "How?"

The man came dangerously close to bowling him over but pulled up just short. His face one of aggression, but then it transformed into calm and in good English he said, "Why are you here?"

"I belong to an excursion party," Irwin stated trying to maintain his calm and project strength. The other Indians now arrived and he could see murder in their faces. The natural impulse to preserve his life at all costs kicked in, "I can tell you were they are."

"Can you show us the way out of these mountains," inquired the calm Indian.

"Yes, I know all the paths and passes," he said with increasing confidence, "There are many hazards, bogs, and rivers to cross but I can guide you in the most direct route out of here."

One of the angrier Indian's pulled up close yelling, "We are heap mad! Where are the others?"

Several other angry warriors pulled up to the group then. To Jim they looked as if they were the worst sort and had nothing but blood on their minds. They began crowding around him. Some were shouting into his face and others jeering and pointing. They all were bumping into his horse with theirs as the group rotated around him like a tornado. From the center of the maelstrom he could see more and more weapons appearing in warriors' hands.

One of them shoved his rifle barrel against Jim's chest yelling, "Give'em me that coat!"

He quickly took it off and handed it to the man, hoping to abate his anger. Now he only wore a rough one of those dirty-gray army shirts made of saddle-blanket material.

"Last I saw," Jim said swallowing hard and pointing, "They were headed over there. There are a couple good camps at the base of that mountain by the creek." He wished he had not said it the moment the words came out but as his pa always said, 'That ship has sailed.' All he could do now was go with the flow and not fight the current or it would sweep him under and that would be his end.

The leader said something to the others in Nez Perce and suddenly they left him alone. The warriors broke off and with whooping and shouting rode the direction Jim had pointed. "Lord, have mercy," he muttered.

"You'em under my protection," the leader said, "You'em goin' guide us all from here."

It appeared the leader had claimed him as a prisoner to be their guide. He was safe, for the moment.[v]

The Helena Party

August 26th

Otter Creek

Andrew Weikert was feeling much better since finishing breakfast. Standing up his body gave a reflexive stretch and his arms reached up high above his head. Andy was a man of slightly thicker build than average and a bit taller as well. He smoothed the wavy dark brown hair beneath his hat. Despite jesting that his hairline had began to run from his eyebrows, he had more hair than other men his age. His thick eyebrows and large moustache made up for his little loss of head hair.

As he took his plate and fork to the washing area it was obvious he was a man of physicality. He had the grace and strength of a man in total control of his body. He stepped easily through camp without effort to avoid trip hazards or find a path.

He couldn't help feeling considerably easier than he had in the past 12 hours. A thought kept bouncing around in his head, "If the Indians wanted to whoop us up they would have attacked us during the night."

He looked over at the other mounted man, Leslie N. Wilkie. Wilkie, like Andy and the rest of the men, sported a large moustache with stubble beginning to fill in the jaw line and chin. The broad brimmed hat resting atop the crown of his head concealed wavy light brown hair that had been cropped close. For being a draughtsman he was athletic like Andy. Nearly a half-head shorter but more stout, the man was able to command a horse well and shoot accurately. He was just the type of man Andy wanted with him on the scouting.

Andy then asked once more if Dietrich, Pfister, or Kneck were sure they did not want to come along. Stewart, Duncan, and Roberts had already declined twice and he didn't feel right asking the 17 year-old Foller or the Negro cook, Stone, whose rheumatism was exacerbated by the morning chill.

The ten men had met in the Park on the 20th to tour the wonders of the north: Mammoth Springs, Tower Falls, Yellowstone Falls, Yellowstone Lake, and the numerous geysers reportedly blanketing the area. Weikert, Roberts, Dietrich, and Pfister had departed Helena Montana on the 13th and after riding 14 miles they spent that night in a one-stall barn at Prickly Pear Ranch.

It was a raucous night and the racket made it so no man could have slept even if he had wanted to. Sometime during the night Pete, one of the packhorses, had pulled up his picket pin and struck out for his old range. So, early in the morning Andy saddled up and caught up to him after a ten-mile ride. Pete had found a band of horses and was happily grazing with them. The long rope trailing from his halter made Pete easy to capture and they were back with the rest of the group by 9:30.

The rest of the trip down was uneventful other than Andy's shotgun being rendered useless the next day. His horse, Toby, had lost its footing and fell down. The snapping sound of his shotgun stock caused the others to wheel their horses towards him. He could tell they had feared a snapped leg by the looks in their eyes and the relief on their faces when he lifted up his shotgun. They travelled between 25 to 35 miles a day for the next 7 days. Then at 2 PM they had arrived at their predetermined meeting spot: Mammoth Hot Springs.

They had caught up to the rest of their touring group: Duncan, Wilkie, and Ben Stone. Two of their group set about making dinner and the other two staked down the tent. Dietrich did not like the bacon brought for supper and had set out for Gardiner's River to catch some fresh trout as an alternative. Weikert, whom the rest of the group called "Andy", had more interest in the natural wonders and had convinced Roberts to

41

take a stroll and look at the hot springs and volcanic formations in the area.

As they wove around the stemming waters and bright colored soils they agreed that reading about the wonders only gave a very faint idea of their true properties. After three hours of touring they had returned to camp. The group ate together before singing a few songs and retiring to bed.

The next day had been nearly the same with one exception. After breakfast a little squabble arose, Dietrich had refused to wash the dishes. The group reminded him that prior to leaving they all had agreed to do what they could towards cooking and helping around camp as well as taking care of their own horses. Dietrich had slowly abdicated his duties to the point of only caring for his own horse. He continued to refuse and they told him that if he was going to be that way he could see to cooking his own grub and washing his own dishes. Dietrich stood up and left for the Springs saying over his shoulder, "I'll wash them when I come back." After he left the others had washed their dishes and left his on the ground. It had been a couple days of active "recuperation" while visiting nearby attractions, the entire group set off for sightseeing the Falls and Geyser Basin.

Andy remembered the vibrant colors and wondrous spectacle of the Falls where they camped on the 23rd. The day had begun as a very fine morning; everything seemed to be alive and birds were singing everywhere. Deer and elk occasionally could be seen skipping about.

They had spent the day exploring the area, touring both the Upper and Lower Falls. At one point the men amused themselves by rolling rocks down into the river far below. Eventually all wearied of the venture and one of them suggested they go down to the river. The men walked the rim back and forth looking for a way into the canyon that contained the raging ribbon of water below. Every attempt failed and even the most promising route required around 250-300 feet of rope for the decent.

They all decided to be content with looking at the scene from the rim. A route to the river at the Lower Falls was found and Andy asked one of the others to hold his feet while he shimmied to the edge of the rock and look over. Andy removed his hat and set it on a branch before lower to his belly and crawling out to the edge. He felt as though someone was trying to push him over the edge but knew that the feeling was not true. Once over the edge he could see the seething waters created where the 300-foot waterfall crashed into the ground below. Clouds of cool mist bellowed upwards but lacked the strength to reach him. The colors of the soil lining the canyon walls were indescribable.

All agreed despite the beauty of the Upper Falls, the Lower Falls were the more spectacular because of the canyon it spilled into.

The next day they had visited Mud Geyser by noon. They crossed Alum Creek not long afterwards. The headwaters of the stream was so strong that one swallow of the astringent-laced water was sufficient to draw a man's face in such a shape that it is impossible to get it straightened again for at least an hour. They pushed on and paused at the crest of the hill. Before them a beautiful prairie stretched for three miles before a spectacular mountain jutted from its surface. Layer after layer of almost entirely pure brimstone stretched 150-foot into the sky. Wisps of steam oozed from all parts of the mountain for its entire 1-mile circumference. They had arrived at Sulphur Mountain.

The group gazed at the impressive sight for as long as they dared. Andy heard someone opine that it was another four miles to the planned campsite and they should move on so they could make supper in the light of day. They all felt the early pangs of hunger coming on and heeled their horses forward.

The scenery was breathtaking. They had ridden in silence interrupted occasionally by exclamations of amazement. After a mile of riding, the morning was coming to a close. Duncan had ridden ahead to reconnoiter. Suddenly he came galloping from the top of the mountain exclaiming, "There's a damn big party of tourists, or else a big band of elk, ahead!"

Wilkie had replied, "Yes, your elk will turn out to be trees, like all the rest of the game you see."

After traveling two or three more miles the men had began to grow uneasy. They could see something alive coming, but did not know what it was. A large moving caravan was moving in the distance.

"I think it is a large group of tourists like us." A voice from Andy's left stated.

They decided to keep riding on to see who it was. Traveling on until reaching the top of a small hill, they paused to observe again. The large caravan was just across the Yellowstone River.

Duncan exclaimed in complete surprise, "Indians! Indians! My God, its Indians!" The Indian's vanguard was now crossing the Yellowstone River. The entire caravan was moving at a lively pace, causing speculation among the tourists.

One of them stated that, "If they are hostile Indians than it likely is Joseph's Nez Perce."

Another added, "Then they are fleeing from Howard which explains their hurried pace."

Andy remarked hopefully, "If they are peaceable Indians then they will go about their business. The only risk of damage would be if they tried to steal our horses."

Duncan added, "I still propose we backtrack to be safe. There are at least 300 warriors that we can see in the Indian caravan. And we number only ten; we wouldn't stand a chance."

There wasn't any disagreement. First one than another spoke his agreement until all had agreed to return the way they had come. One of them suggested a meadow they had crossed by Sulphur Springs about five or six miles back. Another agreed that it was a good spot and still another thought he remembered it as a good, defensible place. They decided to return there, set up camp, and establish a watch during the night. The group traveled back at a very lively rate. A few of the men did not care to check their horses' gait and soon were galloping at full speed.

Having a lead rope in his off-hand, Andy watched as those men pulled further and further ahead.

They had slowed their pace between the forks of the first creek above the upper falls. This was the place the men had been talking about. It felt quite secure and they stopped to discuss their situation. One of the men proposed that they go no farther. Just as they had remembered, the springs were a both beautiful and safe campsite. He also again brought up that if Howard was after the fleeing Indians then by tomorrow they would be gone. The group's scare had seemed to subside a little and all agreed to make camp.

After more deliberation the group had agreed to wait it out. The majority was of the mind to go ahead to the geysers, as they had come this far, and the journey was almost completed. Duncan was the only man who did not want to continue the trip. He suggested they get up early and head out to home. They should put as much distance between them and the Indians as possible. He could not sway the majority and a compromise was settled on. It was decided that in the morning a couple of them would ride out to ascertain the location and disposition of the Indians. If they still saw the Indian village, one of them would fire his rifle and warn the party. Those who stayed behind would break camp and when the two scouts returned they all would leave for home.

Their location was a place that was easily defensible. They set up their tents in a slight depression behind a 20-foot high triangular knoll rising between the forks of Otter Creek. From its top a man could command a view and defense of every approach to the camp. The camp was entirely concealed from all approaches unless the hill was crested. The men unpacked and pitched tents where they had stopped and discussed it.

As the tents were unfurled and the ground cleared Duncan quietly announced he did not feel safe in the meadow. He was going to make his bed in the timber. He gathered up his blankets and headed into the timber. After half a mile he felt more secure and cleared a small sleeping area in the pine needles.

All the men camped there for the night, except the one who was too nervous and wanted to go back home: Duncan. Not feeling safe, he had taken his blankets and made his bed half a mile from camp in the timber. Andy remembered that all of them had laughed at him as he took his bedding and headed off to the timber.

But despite the quite and peacefulness, Andy could not shake his uneasiness. When they finally retired into their tents he was still pretty nervous and could not sleep. His mind would not stop playing scenarios. He kept turning them over and over to increase his preparedness for any eventuality. His mind also had latched onto each and every little forest noise. It had turned them all into an alarm of impending doom. He had strained his sense of hearing to determine if it was a false alarm. Time drug on and he tossed and turned in his bed. Sleep never came to him.

It had been 6 o'clock in the morning when the men finished eating breakfast; the time had come to investigate if the Indians had moved. Andy had volunteered to go check for the Indians and had not been able to sleep for fear of attack. He wore the baggy-eyed mask of a sleepless man and Wilkie did not want his friend to beg for a partner to accompany him. So, after the first request he offered to go with him. The men saddled their horses while joking with the others. Andy double-checked his equipment: his revolver, rifle, telescope, and saddlebags. He said his goodbyes to the other eight men in camp. Turning Toby towards Sulphur Mountain and clicking his tongue, he headed off with Wilkie.

The miles went by more quickly than the day before. Andy had no interest in the scenery around him unless it offered potential concealment. The thought of Indians lurking around deprived him of the ability to drink in the beauty of the park around him as he had the day before. He and Wilkie had tried to talk at first but after a mile or two their conversation slowed and stopped. He couldn't remember which of them had spoken last but one of them had simply not answered the trivial question asked buy the other. But the other had not asked for an answer either. They settled into an uneasy silence and rode with their senses focused on the potential danger ahead.

Soon they reached the place where they had seen the Indians; where the shoulders of two hills converged as if the pair of giant plateaus they belonged to were leaning on each other. Before reaching the crest they dismounted and eased their way to an easy observation point. Andy maneuvered to a place behind a fallen tree and studied the scene below. He heard the slight rustling of brush as Wilkie came up next to him. What they saw lightened their moods. The Indians had moved on, leaving a trail on the far shoulder, headed away from the Geyser Basin. The entire village had been dismantled and was on the move.

"By the end of the morning they would be far enough away for us to be safe in packing up and continuing our trip," Andy stated with growing excitement and relief.

"It looks like the coast is clear," Wilkie replied, "I wonder how far we can make before camp tonight?"

"I'd be willing to bet we could tour down to Yellowstone Lake and camp there tonight," Andy replied, his face and body more visibly relaxed.

"I think your right, but only if we get back straight away and the boys pack up quickly!"

Still keeping low, they returned to their horses. As Andy swung into his saddle he felt lightness returning to his mood. He sawed his Toby around and they started back at a much brisker pace.

The good news buoyed their spirits and they light-heartedly talked as they rode southeast back to camp. The golden orb of the sun had fully risen, only accompanied in the sky by a few high cirrus clouds feathered across the cobalt blue canvas. It was another beautiful morning. The air was filled with birds singing and squirrels chattering. Andy's feeling of fear had dissolved and he allowed the sun to warm face and to enjoy the wilderness around him. It was an exquisite landscape!

Andy was in the lead and he decided to circle towards the Yellowstone River and go around the knobby hill that separated them from camp. He paused to at the crest of a fold in the ground. It was a good view of the surrounding land and he drank in the sight as Wilkie caught up to him.

"What is that?"

Andy followed his friend's pointer finger to a small dark shape on the prairie about a mile away, "A stray horse it appears."

"Yes, it looks like an Indian pony. Let's go catch it and take it back to camp."

Andy looked at his friend sideways.

"It will be for luck!" Wilkie stated as he flashed a smile and heeled his horse towards the pony.

Andy followed his friend and let the brisk morning air rejuvenate his spirit. He took a slightly different route to head off the pony if it changed position from where they first spotted it.

He kept his eyes fixed on the animal as they closed in on it. The pony lifted its head from grazing and looked at them for a moment before returning to feeding. Andy could see now that it was just a colt.

"It is fairly young, hopefully it had been trained to lead," he said as he slid his hand over to the rope tied to the side of his saddle and removed it.

The colt shied away from Wilkie, who was closer because of his head start. They both talked gently to calm it. It lifted its head and began to walk away. Andy readied his rope and as the colt moved towards him he swung his rope once, twice, and then let it fly. It was a perfect thrown! The rope landed around the colts head and slid down its neck. It reacted with fear and flinched, jerking its head backwards. It did not like the feel of the rope and shook its head and neck to free itself.

"Nice throw, let's lead it back to camp." Wilkie exclaimed as he moved up to Andy.

With a click of his tongue and leaning forward in the saddle Andy urged Toby forward. Now for the moment of truth! They moved until the rope was played out and became taut on the colt. Not only did not it not follow but it pulled back against the rope!

The men tried to coax it with gentle tones and clicking their tongues. But it was to no avail; the colt was becoming wild-eyed. It snorted with irritation and commenced kicking its hind legs as it crow-hoped in a semicircle. Clods of prairie mud were flying in all directions and the men's horses were becoming skiddish too. Before Andy could wind the near end of the rope around his saddle horn the colt gave a mighty heave with his neck and jerked the rope loose.

"Let's try driving it!" Wilkie suggested as he turned his horse to face the bucking colt.

They used their best cowboying skills to direct and drive the colt. They cut and pushed as a team but the wily little colt would have none of it. It darted between them or made long arcs around their sides. It was forcing them to drive it the wrong direction.

After a quarter hour or so of struggling with the young animal they paused for a breather and looked at each other.

Andy spoke first, "This is not the type of 'luck' I want in our camp!"

Wilkie shook his head, "I couldn't agree more. Let's get your rope and head back."

Andy rode over to the colt, which was close to exhaustion, and tried to retrieve his rope. The animal allowed him to grab the loose end but once he tried to approach it to loosen the loop around its neck the animal began to kick and buck again. This time Andy was prepared and quickly wound the his end of the rope around his saddle horn.

The colt would not calm down and after several minutes Wilkie rode up and shouted, "I think we'll have to choke it down to get your rope!"

Andy had tried to avoid doing that but could see it was the only option now. He positioned Toby and backed him up so the rope tightened on the colt's neck and cut off it's airflow. It pulled against him to try and free itself and sped up the process. When it finally toppled over, Andy quickly dismounted and removed his rope.

"We've wasted enough time here," he said as he swung into his saddle.

"Let's get back to camp, maybe we can still make Yellowstone Lake before night if there are no more Indian sightings!"

They head towards the Yellowstone River at a brisk pace. When they hit it, the men paralleled south along its churning waters for over a mile. Andy had calmed down from the colt fiasco and was again enjoying the wilderness around him.

Approaching the place where the Alum Creek disgorged itself to join the river's flow to Yellowstone Lake, they knew that they were nearing camp. They turned their horses up the creek and passed through a stand of timber. Coming into a glade that descended into a small oval meadow, Andy let Toby have its head.

Wilkie was a few rods behind him on the trail and Andy turned to talk with him. From the corner of his eye caught movement down the hill. It instantly registered; it was the heads of Indians bobbing up from behind a fallen tree. He had rode within a mere 75 yards of the log; it was an ambush!

His eyes widened with fear and he yelled, "Indians!" With his left hand he jerked the reigns to wheel Toby around in a circle and simultaneously readied his rifle with the right. As Toby was completing the circle and his rifle was coming to his shoulder Andy was looking back at the no less than a half dozen rifles leveled at him from behind the log.

This instantly changed his plan and he played "Injun." He made himself as small as he could by hugging down on the neck of Toby, with his gun across his knees. Andy again turned Toby toward around but it resisted his efforts; it knew they were headed back to camp and did not understand why he suddenly wanted to change course.

A trio of rifle reports and bullets zipping past gave Toby his answer. They also sent it hopping in surprise and panic. No projectiles struck them but Andy was at risk for losing any control of Toby.

Andy yanked his reigns to turn Toby after Wilkie. He saw a half-dozen more rifles heading to shoulders as he finally wrest control of him and spun around. He spurred him mercilessly in the ribs to follow Wilkie. Apparently his friend had been able to turn around at his first shout.

A cluster of gunfire erupted behind him. In the same moment, Andy felt the unmistakable punch of a bullet as it sliced a four-inch long cut along and tore a chip out of his shoulder blade. It knocked him forward against his saddle horn but he maintained his seat. Now in full gallop, Toby leapt a dry seasonal creek bed. As it gained the other side another barrage of fire erupted and again Andy felt the slap of a bullet; this time it had ripped a chunk from the stock of his rifle. He hugged even closer to Toby's neck but there was no more room to flatten himself.

Another volley was unleashed at him; the bullets came fast and thick. But he had made it to the end of their rifles' accuracy range and the bullets slapped into the tree branches all around him but too far away to cause great concern. He seemed to be making his escape! Many of the Indian's were running for their horses; "Now time for a race!" thought Andy.

But just then Toby caught his hoof on the lip of the embankment and nearly turned a somersault. Andy was thrown forward over the neck of his mount and sent sprawling on the ground in front of his horse. His shoulder wound exploded with pain but he heard the Indians running up for a shot at him and knew he hadn't the time to placate his wound.

"My horse is shot! My only chance is to get behind one of those trees and turn my repeater loose on the redskins," Andy instantly thought.

But just at that moment Toby rolled over and tried balancing itself back on its feet again. He had maintained a grip on the reigns in the left hand by pulling them over its head in the fall! Using his repeater, Andy let loose with a round of his own at the charging warriors. They dodged for cover and he spun to Toby, who had just gained his feet. With reigns in one hand and his gun in the other, he put a hand on the horn and leapt into the saddle. He was off to the races again! All this happened is a few seconds.

He thought that sending another round at the ambushers was a good idea and twisted around. As he turned in the saddle to take the parting shot at his adversaries, he began to raise the gun. It had barely moved when a flash of movement caught his eye, just as a limb from a nearby tree caught his face! It smacked him hard just beneath the ear, the rough bark tearing at his flesh. He saw a flash of bright lights and felt the sting of the scrapes furrowed across his jaw. He registered his hat flying off to the side. Andy decided that he could do very well without his hat at this stage of the game and didn't even think of attempting its retrieval.

It took all his strength to stay in his seat but he did. And a glance back showed the Indians staring with mouths gapping. Surprise at his speedy departure was written across all their faces. His mind also noted that they had no ponies nearby so he would have a good head start on them!

He raced towards Wilkie who was quirting his horse towards a stand of timber up Alum Creek. The distance was significant, as he has gotten considerably ahead of Andy. He urged the most possible speed from Toby and was making up ground quickly. The wind rushed past him and he squinted his eyes to avoid tears from the dryness. The only sound he heard was the thumping of his heart downing out his horse's heavy breathing and the wind rushing past. He dared not look back at their pursuers as he used the ends his reigns to ply the greatest sped from Toby as possible. He had nearly caught up to him as the pair broke over a low ridge and then raced across the prairie along Alum Creek in the valley. Andy followed him back towards the timber again and they started to slow their horses. He caught up with Wilkie as they neared the timber and he looked back but saw no Indians pursuing them.

They entered the timber and slowed their mounts from a full gallop. Ducking branches and exercising their best horsemanship skills, they wove in and out of the trees with the fastest trot safety allowed. Soon the forest underbrush choked the forest floor and the branches were too numerous to dodge. The low branches whipped at Andy's face and he took a pine bough to the mouth.

"I'm dismounting," he announced.

Just ahead Wilkie was battling the vegetation as well. He dismounted also and led his horse through on foot. Andy gave him a slight lead before plunging in after him. This way the supple young branches would not whip back and hit Andy in the face. After penetrating the timber for quite a distance, Wilkie halted and turned around.

He asked, "Are you hurt?"

"Judging from the hole in my shirt on the right shoulder and the way the blood is running in my boot, I think I must have a scratch at least. How about you?"

"No. I was too far off. They mostly shot at you. Turn around and let's look at your shoulder." He replied gesturing for Andy to turn his back to him.

After Andy turned there was a moment's pause before Wilkie added, "Oh yes, you *did* get a scratch and then some. We need to bandage it and then warn the others. Hopefully the Indians have not been to camp yet!"

He nodded agreement to his friend's statement, "We've got to warn the others!" Andy pulled the arm from his sleeve and slid the shirt over the shoulder to expose the wound. He waited as Wilkie tore cloth into strips and dressed his wound as best he could.

When he finished, Wilkie suggested, "We need to check the horses too."

Pulling his shirt back on he turned to Toby. The two men both thoroughly examined their mounts. Running their hands under the blankets and around tack blocking their views they found no sign of injury; they were both sound mounts still. They thanked God for that not-so-small fortune and led the horses from the thick brush.

Swinging into the saddle Wilkie pointed towards camp, "I think that's our most direct path."

Andy nodded in agreement and pointing that direction they spurred their horses and rode as lively as they could. Andy shouted over to his friend, "I hope the Indians had not discovered camp yet!"

"Then we can warn the others before calamity befalls them," Wilkie agreed.

As they broke out of the forest and onto the trail Andy recognized they were pretty near camp.

The light of day filtered by the forest slowly increased as the pair neared the meadow where the camp was set. It was eerily silent.

"The boys must have heard the Indians shooting at us." Andy offered hopefully.

"Yes, then packed up and struck out for other quarters." Wilkie added hopefully but not convincingly.

They saw nothing moving at the camp, no men and no horses. It was completely deserted. The men looked at each other, knowing what they would likely find, but hoping to be wrong.

Andy began shouting, "Hello! Hello!"

They had begun to fear the worst when no replies came.

Wilkie joined his salutation and they closed the distance to the camp.

Andy broke into the glade first. His fears were confirmed; they had been too late.[vi] They had not given the warning that they were supposed to and the camp was in shambles, his friends possibly dead. He forced down the anger rising in him and looked to Wilkie. His face showed the same mix of guilt and anger that he felt.

They locked eyes for a moment before Andy suggested, "We must check for survivors before the Indians come back."

They rode in ever-widening concentric circles around the camp. He could not see any bodies on the ground. "Perhaps our friends all escaped?" Andy said hopefully.

"Without bodies I think you may be right, since we found no blood or bodies," Wilkie agreed, "lets go back to camp and see what we can find."

They headed back to camp hopeful. It looked like a tornado had torn through it. All the tents, blankets, and all 14 horses were missing. The campfire had been piled with fishing gear, extra clothing, personal items, and whatever else the Indians had not wanted to take. It made a large smoldering pile in the center of what once was camp.

Several shotguns, unwanted by the Indians, lay splintered upon the ground. The shattered wooden stocks on one side and the barrels on the other side of a tree where the horses had been kept told the story. The Indians had gripped the barrels and they had swung the weapons against the tree breaking them.

"If it weren't for that colt on the prairie we would have been here during the attack," Andy spoke a realization aloud.

Wilkie shook his head, "I thought that too. Let's get food and other necessary supplies and get out of here."

Andy dismounted and walked over to where their larder had been. The larder area had been thoroughly ransacked; only spilled flour, crackers and some beans remained strewn on the ground. "Nothing here, they took almost all of it."

"Here as well," Wilkie reported from the cooking preparation area.

Andy nodded to the smoldering pile of items on the fire, "Let's check there." He grabbed a stick and pulled a coat from the top of the smoky mess. Fishing poles had been snapped over knees and the tackle was reduced to glowing orange piles of twisted metal. Coats and clothing reeked of smoke and nearly all had sizable holes throughout. They tried picking through the smoldering pile for a few moments before abandoning it to its fate. Everything was far too smoky or burned to be of good use.

"There were a few cracker pieces we might salvage," Andy opined.

They headed back to the food area. Both men stooped down and picked out the large pieces of crackers. They found the few that were not filthy and continued their search for food.

Wilkie walked to the other side of the fire and spotted a canvas sack that appeared to rest atop something. He stepped over and flipped the sack off with the toe of his boot. Sure enough something had been missed. Under the canvas sack he discovered a pot that contained an uncooked ham! It had been knocked over in the flight of their friends and missed by the Indians. "The boys must have been taken completely by surprise," said Andy stepping over to him.

He stepped over and grabbed a partially burned burlap sack. Taking the pot he dumped the hunk of meat into the sack and grabbed a piece of rope from the edge of the fire. He securely tied the bundle to his saddle horn.

Wilkie had been looking through the wreckage more closely. "There is nothing more to take."

"Were do you think survivors would go?"

"I suspect they would likely make their way back to McCartney's hotel at The Springs," Wilkie offered.

"That's 50 miles away. But, I think that is the most likely rendezvous spot." They swung back into their saddles and headed that direction.

"Let's keep to the timber," Andy suggested.

They did just that, struck through the timber and going slow enough to keeping a sharp eye out for the Indians. They had made a good distance when the trees began to thin and then patches of prairie broke the forest into smaller and smaller islands of evergreen trees. Then the men emerged from the forest and broke into pure prairie. Andy saw movement down the line of timber. His heart jumped and he readied his gun.

Wilkie had noticed at the same time and exclaimed, "A bear!" It was racing out of the timber too but quite a distance off. Andy relaxed and they watched as it continued loping towards them. It was looking around but seeming oblivious to their presence.

As it was closing in still unaware of them Andy asked, "Should we chase it down and shoot it?"

"I think not, our horses have been under saddle all day already," Wilkie replied regretfully.

" You're right. And it will be morning at best when we arrive at the hotel" added Andy.

"Should we warn it," Andy asked.

"It is getting too close for my comfort! I think a warning shot is worth the risk of alerting the Indians," Wilkie exclaimed with increasing urgency as the predator was quickly closing the distance between them.

Andy pointed his rifle in the bear's general direction and fired off a round. At the sound of the shot, the bear stopped dead in its tracks and spun around so quickly Andy almost. It tore off back in the direction it had come but at a much faster pace.

Prudence had won out. They turned their horses back the direction of the hotel. Wilkie heeled his horse down the trail. Nervous about having alerted the Indians, Andy shoved another cartridge into his gun and then spurred his horse to a trot after Wilkie.

They constantly searched ahead and around for signs of their attackers. At the same time they needed to put distance between them and the Indians and make descent time to make the hotel by night so they kept a faster pace than allowed good reconnoitering.

They had not traveled very far when Wilkie raised his hand and said urgently, "Wait! There are men ahead on the trail!"

Andy rode next to him and followed his finger to a distant hill where a couple men walked leading a horse in the direction of the hotel.

Andy studied the scene before saying, "I can make out a horse and two men, but no details."

"The horse has no saddle."

"You're right. They might be Indians."

Andy twisted in the saddle and reached back to his saddle bags. After retrieving his field glasses and putting them to his eyes he studied the group more, "Well, they aren't red men anyhow." He said as he lowered and handed them to Wilkie.

Wilkie took them and studied for a long moment too. "No, but I can't make out who they are. Let's overtake them and find out." Handing the glasses back, he heeled his mount forward at a gallop.

Andy followed close behind. They overtook the dismounted travelers much faster than Andy had expected. As he came up from behind, he saw the men were walking painfully slow. The one leading the horse had a pronounced limp to one side whereas the other man hobbled forward crippled in general misery; they were averaging a pace of 35 feet a minute.

As they drew still nearer, Andy recognized the men. The overcoat on the limping man belonged to Stewart and the hobbling man was Stone. "Hallo there!" He shouted and urged Toby to greater speed.

The men turned in fear at first then in anticipation as their names quickly followed, "Stewart, Stone hold up!"

Andy leaned from his saddle as Toby skidded to a stop mere feet from the men. He pumped each man's hand with exuberance while smiling broadly. They returned his smile and handshake in the same vain and exchanged pleasantries with Wilkie as well. They all shared in the jubilation of finding alive friends believed dead.

They quickly exchanged stories of what happened at camp and any knowledge of the other friends' fates. Apparently the men in camp completely ignored the natural advantages of the camp's position; no one was atop the knoll as a guard. This in fact turned the natural advantage of the terrain into a natural disadvantage as the Indians had used its cover to approach under the cover of the hill unnoticed. They had crept up its sides and exploded over the crest nearly in camp before the men knew what was happening.

Ben related, "I been kindling da fire to git dinnah and the rest ob the men were lounging about relaxing. There was a couple shots ober our direction. Well, they was so far off the mark I figured it had to be you two firin' at us to scare us. I didn't seed anyone so I shouted, 'You can't scare us!' and den a second volley come crashin' down on us. I dun looked around to see the rest of dem all taking to da brush.' I dun thinked it was high time to git myself. An' I dropped eberyting an' bolted trew de bushes, I dun. Tall running I dun an' wit balls all 'bout me. I dun made the crick and thar dun I stay. I dun seed de Injuns lookin' all 'bout de camp an' crick an' pears like dey mighty anxious to fine me, but I wasen't anxious to fine dem. So I dun went deeper in da weeds."

Stewart then spoke, "They gave us a complete surprise. When the shooting started I was with Kenck and we bolted into the timber. The Indians followed us up and commenced a barrage of fire. I was hit in the side and the calf of the leg. I saw Kenck still running as I fell. I heard a few more volleys but don't know if they got him or if he made good his escape."

"How did you make it out," Wilkie inquired.

"Not long after the final fusillade the Indians came back to me…" Stewart spat with a mix of shame and disgust, "I begged them to spare my life. The nearest me seemed disposed to just kill me but the pair behind him pushed his gun down and asked in good English if I had any money. I told them there was $200 in my back pocket. They rolled me over and liberated the roll of money and my silver watch too. I still believed that they were going to kill me. They stepped away and had a big medicine talk. They spoke in their native tongue but I could tell they were discussing whether or not to let me live. After what felt like an eternity one of them stepped over and said, 'You can live.' Then they left me. After I couldn't see them I began to drag myself to the creek. I pulled myself to the bank and washed my wounds. By the time I finished I could see the Indians had finished with our camp and were ready to start. It was then that my mare was coming to me. I called to her and she came up. The Indians had gone by then so I got a halter and put it on her."

"Amazing! Isn't this the same horse that you've always had to keep a 40 foot rope on to catch," Andy questioned.

"Yes! But this morning she behaved and I led her to a log and crawled on her. I rode her for around a mile but my wounds hurt too much for me to stay on. I had to dismount and lead her.

"Around that time Stone came hobbling along. I'm sure his rheumatism affliction was done no good by standing in freezing water."

"Dats true, mine bones all were lockin' up!"

"It was a wonder that anyone escaped," exclaimed Wilkie.

"No doubt! What of the other men", Andy asked.

"I couldn't say. We all were running for our lives last I saw." Stewart replied sourly.

"I dunno, I seed nothin' ob dem Andy." Stone signed.

Wilkie spoke up, "The place to discuss this is not the middle of the prairie."

Andy looked around, "Agreed," he nodded at Stewart, "Why aren't you riding your horse?"

"Without a saddle and stirrups I cannot control my body's bounce. Each step of the horse was agony. Every time her hoof struck ground I was driven onto my buttock which shoved my hipbone into my wounded side."

"Did you try to squeeze tighter with your legs," Wilkie asked.

"I did. But the moment I tried that the wound in my calf throbbed with unbearable pain. Each squeeze was worsened it; I feel much better just walking. Since it was less painful to walk when I came across Stone, I decided to dismount and walk."

Andy probed again, "Ben why didn't you just ride instead?"

Ben replied, "Dat icy water. I jus' wa' all stiff an' locked up. Eben if he dun helped me on the hoss dar waz no way ob me stayin' on widout a saddle."

Andy and Wilkie immediately swung down off their horses. "At your current pace we would take far too long to reach the hotel," Andy stated matter of factly.

There was no discussion of some riding ahead and sending back help. "We will stay together and face what comes as a group," Wilkie added.

Andy stepped back and sized up the horses and the other men, "Maybe if Stewart used the stirrups to bear his bodyweight."

Wilkie shook his head in agreement and finished the thought, "Then he might be able to absorb the bouncing of the horse."

Stewart limped over to look at the rigs on each horse, "I believe that would work just fine. Let's give it a try!"

"I think Toby's rig might work," Andy offered.

"But the stirrups look a little longer and seat a little wider than mine," Wilkie opined.

"I think your right," agreed Andy after looking again more closely. "Lets position him over there," he added pointing up the trail a few rods. "We can use that series of small boulders to give him an advantage to mount."

Stewart hobbled over to rocks as Wilkie led his horse into position. Stewart used them like stairs as Andy held his right arm for balance. He assisted him onto Wilkie's saddle and then turned back to retrieve Toby as the other horse was led away.

Wilkie handed the reigns to Stewart and returned to their makeshift stairs. Toby was led to the same position as Wilkie's horse and they called Ben over. When he was there Andy took one arm and Wilkie the other, they gave the stiff and weary Ben Stone a lift onto Andy's horse.

Ben groaned and tried to settle in. "I think dis will do jus' fine," he finally stated.

With the two most-injured men mounted they turned their sights to Mount Washburn, the main obstacle in their path to the hotel and relative safety. The trail cut through the open prairie climbing up and then down the small rolling hills that gradually rose and joined together to become the steep 10,200-foot peak that was the men's main natural obstruction to the hotel.

They travelled just fine for several miles; Stewart was able to bear the pain by using the stirrups as suggested. Andy noticed that Stone seemed to sit gingerly on the saddle as well. Looking more closely he noticed a tear in the man's britches at his bottom. "Stone, how'd you get your pants torn?" He questioned.

"Where?" Stone replied baffled.

"On the behind," Andy said pointing to the location on himself.

Stone twisted in the saddle and searched until finding the place. "I know where I got that now; dat was when I fell. I recollect it feeling as tho' something was trying to crawl under me and here it was a piece of lead!" He further explained, "When the injuns all had commenced der shootin' at me, I 'ad run 'bout 200 yards with dem shootin' before I dun felled into da crick, liken I told ya. The grass and reeds was quite tall so I laid der fur three or four 'ours 'til dem all left. Dat crawlin' feeling hit me right den. I 'posed they think dem had killed old Ben and neber went to me."

Focusing on the trail Andy and Ben became lost in their own thoughts.

They quietly walked at a pretty lively pace for some time. Each man was intent upon the ups and downs of the day, replaying their near-death encounters to themselves and wondering about their missing friends. They hoped they all had escaped as well. No one had actually seen another man die so there was still hope that they had bribed their way out like Stewart or hid their way out like Stone.

The quartet continued like this for several miles. Stewart broke the introspective silence with a proclamation, "I'm feeling faint. I need to get down. If I dismount and rest for a couple hours I'll be ready again."

Andy looked pointedly at Wilkie who shook his head "no" in agreement; stopping was a very bad idea. They both knew that if Stewart dismounted they would get no further that night.

Andy replied, We will stop at the next creek for a water break. Just keep holding on."

"Okay, the next creek," Stewart agreed through gritted teeth.

They traversed a couple of folds in the hills before descending one where a small creek of clear water gurgled past. Without pausing for Stewart, Andy told Toby to follow Wilkie. He then stepped over to the bubbling ribbon of clear water. Stepping over to a pool with fast flowing water spilling into it he submerged the opening and watched the air bubble from the container's mouth as the liquid rushed inside. After he had gathered the water in his canteen, he caught up to his friend. Lifting the canteen to him Andy said, "Here drink this!"

As the horse continued to plod along Stewart took a long pull of the water and looked at Andy and insisted, "I need to get off the horse and bathe my wounds. They are on fire!"

Andy continued walking next to the horse and talking to distract him from the idea. This was demanding work because Andy's mind was consumed by the pain in his shoulder and he could think of little else. Soon Stewart dropped the subject and they had passed from the little gulley.

The grade slowly increased and the horses slowed considerably, laboring heavily to haul their loads up the mountainside. The timber was now consigned to small pockets where moisture had accumulated and the surrounding terrain was the classic Yellowstone volcanic high-altitude desert.

Andy could see the peak of the mountain ahead. It was the frustrating illusion of mountain travel: it grew larger with each mountain bench they ascended but never seemed to be the one that led over the summit. Rise after rise passed, dashing the men's hope they had reached the downhill portion. Finally, they broke out onto a bench and saw it stretch all the way to the mountain's knobby summit.

"Let's stop after the summit and eat." Wilkie suggested.

There was no argument and after pushing beyond the last quarter mile of open ground they gained the other side of the mountain. Stretching before them were the rolling benches of the mountain. Andy traced in his mind the memory of benches eventually tapering into the sage-covered foothills beyond but the moonless night had already settled in enough to prevent him seeing it with his physical eyes.

There was little talk as the men were helped off the horses. Stewart looked Andy square in the eyes as he was lifted from the saddle, "Thanks Andy. I am feeling much better now."

Andy nodded and stepped over to his saddle horn.

While Andy untied the ham and began to cut thin slices from it, Wilkie gathered the little bit of cracker crumbs they had taken from camp. The sliced meat and crumbs were distributed, as meager rations as they were. The men ate in silence, keeping a watchful eye about them. Even Stewart did not object when they stood and returned to the horses. Andy found a suitable set of logs and he and Wilkie mounted the injured men and started off down the trail again. The downhill grade felt better but Andy's feet and legs hurt too much to call it a "good" feeling.

As they began the long descent of Mount Washburn the sun dipped behind the Summit behind them. Shadows of the trees and rocks stretched long before them, some creating hair-raising shapes across the plains ahead of the men. Andy found it was difficult to not see the shapes of Indians lurking behind trees or brush. He was not alone in this as many a time a man gasped and reflexively reached for a gun or ducked in his saddle only to let out a large breath and mutter that it was nothing. The men pushed on with an increased vigor in their stride, an odd mix of fear and hope driving them on.

Stone complained to Andy, "My hoss ain't ke'p hisself up, Andy. Won't ya walk behind em 'cause Ib beginnin' to grow 'fraid ob gitin' left behind an' lost in de dark."

Andy looked back at Toby. Sure enough the animal was lagging behind and stepping sloppily. Stopping to let him walk ahead, Andy calculated that his poor horse was getting tired because he had travelled all day and at a lively pace for the majority of it.

The line of men trudged methodically down the mountain trail slapping one foot in front of the other. The trail was fairly distinct. But on the occasions it faded too much they navigated by starlight in the crisp clear sky.

August 27th

Mammoth Hot Springs, Yellowstone Park

Andy was forcing one foot in front of the other, walking in a rhythm set earlier that morning during the cold darkness preceding dawn. The sun rose in front of the four men, lifting the darkness from the nocks and crannies of the forest. The birds had begun to talk in earnest. The tree squirrels chattered at the line of men when they came too close for the rodents' comfort. Little else was heard in the timber as the coolness of night was driven away by the warmth of the sun's rays.

Andy was pulled from his slumberous march by the chattering of squirrels down the trail, far too distant for them to be the cause. His hand readied his gun and he saw some of the other men raise their heads in alarm as well. Someone or something was on the trail in front of them!

They quickly checked their weapons and were getting to cover when a white man rounded the corner of the trail. He was headed their direction and nearly stumbled into them. Had he been a band of Indians it would have been disastrous!

Wilkie raised his hand in friendship, "Good mornin'!"

The man was startled and replied with a perfunctory, "Good morning!"

"What's your business and how is it you are this deep into the forest at this early hour of the morning," Andy politely inquired.

"I had just left McCartney's Hotel at the Mammoth Springs."

"How far away are we?" Stewart hopefully interjected.

"About ten miles back I'd say," the man replied.

He turned to face Andy again, "I was taking my morning meal when a man named Pfister busted through the door. He said he was part of a tourist group. They had been attacked in their camp by Indians. I was gathering my things to warn prospectors in the hills that hostile Indians were going through that way. Before I could depart two ladies, Mrs. Emma Cowan and Ida Carpenter, and their brother Frank Carpenter showed up at the Springs. They too had been part of a different tourist group that had been attacked. They had been taken captive by the Indians for two days before being released. They had walked past Pfister's group early in the morning but didn't notice them. Otherwise they would have warned them in time." He then pointed looked from face to face before saying, "I'm planning to keep a watch out. I suggest you do the same."

Andy replied bitterly, "We already had a run-in with the Indians. Pfister was part of our group."

"We are headed to the Springs to find any other survivors," Wilkie added, "Safe travel and God's speed."

The man tipped his hat and in moments disappeared around the bend they had just turned. Andy clicked his tongue at Toby and they started off towards the hotel once more.

The ten miles passed quickly. When the men began to recognize where they were they could not help but to quicken their pace. The sun was no longer struggling to climb over the Rocky Mountain peaks and it spilled its golden rays throughout the little valley that housed the Mammoth Hot Springs and the hotel next to it.

A couple of chinked-log buildings sat nestled where the folds of two deciduous tree-choked hillsides converged. At the center of the convergence rose a round rise of earth like a bubble of sediment that was pushing to break free of the stratum that trapped it. Atop the small knoll was a single story log cabin with a lone entry door set between two 12-panel glass windows. Just behind that building stood the log barn and stable. A couple of small bathhouses sat on the periphery of the enormous calcium carbonate formations. A few wooden aqueducts fed thermal water from the springs into the crude little structures.

This was McCartney's hotel; this is where they hoped that their other friends would escape to. Andy checked his watch; it was just before 6 AM. He, Wilkie, and their horses had traveled over 50 miles in just 13 hours! They were all exhausted but still approached the hotel at a lively rate; the knowledge that safety and rest were just ahead blocked the pain and masked the fatigue they all felt.

Andy was almost in a delirious state; on top of all the walking, riding, and blood loss; he had not slept in over 48 hours. He had been too nervous the night before the attack to get any sleep and then they pushed their march through last night.

Now everything was slowed in his mind and action required extreme efforts to initiate and perform. He felt like he was in that euphoric but clumsy state one gets after drinking too much whiskey. He had to force his eyelids to stay open and the world seemed to reel and sway with too fast a head movement.

The trail opened into the valley floor and the hotel was clearly visible. Andy could see movement all around it but his impaired vision was too severe to make out much more than they were white people. One came running towards them and Andy's slow brain registered it was Pfister before he arrived.

Pfister enthusiastically greeted his friends, "Hello! Hello! By God your safe, I feared to be the only one!"

"How did you manage it," Wilkie asked with a genuine smile.

Pfister's eyes lit up, "I had headed away from camp to gather wood for it was nearing dinnertime. Some of the boys were asleep and the remainder were sitting about the campfire. I was busy getting wood when all of the sudden, pop, pop, went the guns and I heard the Indians' yip! Yip! I looked around and saw the camp full of Indians with the boys jumping and going in every direction. I saw two of the boys coming towards me and I lit out for the river. I reached the river and on looking back heard two shots and someone exclaim, 'Oh, my God?'

"I don't know who these two where but think it was Jack Stuart and Kenk. I swam the river, came down to Baronett's bridge, recrossed to this side, and arrived at the junction to find the cavalry. I did't think any of the boys got away. The Indians piled the bullets in plenty. Boy, am I relieved to see you all! Do you thin others made it out?"

He futher explained, "A few hours after my arrival Emma Cowan and Ida and Frank Carpenter had stumbled into camp. They too had been attacked by the Indians."

Pfister now noticed the dried blood on Andy's shoulder and Stewart's leg. "There is an Englishman at the hotel who is a physician," he announced ran off to bring the man over to treat his friends.

"The man hardly took a breath," Andy smiled.

He watched as everyone began hurrying about now. They either were preparing breakfast for the men or preparing dressings for their wounds. Pfister was with a well-dressed man walking towards them. He sat a black bag down at their feet and told Andy in a thick English accent, "Kindly pull that shirt off your shoulder."

Andy complied and grimiced as the dried blood that had soaked through the bandage and onto his shirt ripped open the wound anew. He could feel the blood running down his shoulder again. The doctor introduced himself but Andy could tell he was not interesting in talking and was only trying to distract him. This suited Andy just fine. He had no energy to talk. He winched and loudly sucked in his breath as the man shoved a probe into the wound entrance and ran the blunt end of the probe around the bone. When it touched the bone Andy felt as though a giant sliver of wood was stabbing his flesh. He then moved the probe to the wound's exit.

The doctor continued droning on about nothing. Suddenly it was over. The doctor pulled out the probe and announced, "The ball exited cleanly. I found not cloth either. I will dress it and you should be fine."

He pulled strips of linen and finished dressing Andy's wounds with the precision of an experienced professional. Then he moved on to Ben. Seeing the location he pointed to the nearest shed, "Let's go there to be out of sight of the women." He left to work on cleaning Ben's buttock wound and Andy wanted to look for food.

Before he could stand, a plate was held out to him. Andy ate the breakfast handed him and almost immediately began feeling much better. He finished the food quickly and then looked for a place to take a nap. He spied a sunny spot of green grass away from the hustle and bustle of those around him but close enough to be within their circle of protection.

Someone had taken and cared for Toby so Andy only needed to look to his own needs. He staggered over to the patch of grass and lowered himself down. It was an awkward descent; his body was stiff and achy all over and his shoulder smarted if he bore any weight on that arm. He eased onto his back and closed his eyes.

The sleep he had yearned for the past day did not come easily. In fact it did not come at all. This surprised Andy; he had thought that the moment his eyes closed he would be fast asleep. Unfortunately he was *too* tired to sleep and when his eyes shut he could not stop worrying about the two boys: Roberts and Foller. Their parents looked to him for their kids' safe return and no one knew anything about their fate. Andy tried to focus his mind on the warmth of the sunrays on his face; but his mind seemed to have an agenda of its own. No amount of willpower could keep him from worrying about those boys. And so he was fully awake when the footsteps approached him.

He knew it was Duncan from the sound of his voice even before he opened his eyes to look at the man speaking to him. Duncan's hat was off revealing a long forehead with a small tuft of hair at the center. This patch was stubbornly refusing to retreat back with the rest of Duncan's hair and in the current sweaty presentation gave the man an odd look. Duncan also sported a moustache and goatee but this morning it was starting to look more like a Vandyke because of the growth since their trip began.

"Good Morning Andy. Glad you made it!" The man looked as tired as Andy knew he should feel and neither of them had the energy for much of a reunion.

In fact, as the man collapsed next to him he told Andy, "Dietrich is lying on the trail about two miles out. He was too tired to continue. I told him to stay by the trail and that I would bring help.

"Andy, I am too worn out to fetch him," he mumbled. "Will you go bring him in?"

Andy didn't hesitate, "You bet. Where did you leave him?" He listened carefully as Duncan described a small glade and what the spot he left Dietrich looked like. Andy asked a couple clarifying questions before standing back up on his stiff legs. His entire body protested. But Dietrich was a good friend and Andy wouldn't even have even left an enemy lying out there that morning.

Andy walked over to the hotel stable and he got Toby and a spare horse and saddled them. Toby was played out and Andy did not feel right about asking more from him today but leaving a man out on the trail was not an option. Grabbing his tack he bridled and saddled Toby. Talking softly and patting his trusty horse he promised him that they would be back soon to rest. He swung into the saddle against his aching muscles and led the other horse out of the stable.

Soon the hotel disappeared around the bend behind him. The sun and the slight breeze felt good on his face and in his hair. He was alone but his heightened awareness kept him company; vigilance was his companion on this hopefully short excursion. The trail snaked its way across the high plains desert into the stands of timber hugging the side of the mountain in front of him. He surmised that if he could not sleep at least he was able to help Dietrich.

Andy was approaching the place indicated by Duncan when he saw Dietrich on the trail. The man was unmistakable. He had a slight build on a small frame. His hair parted in the middle of his hairline and he had the look of a delicate city-man rather than a more robust frontiersman.

From the description Andy had been given it appeared he had not moved since Duncan had left him hours ago, not even an attempt to better conceal himself from potential Indians roving about! Andy was not surprised; the man was music teacher in Helena and was not accustom to such hardships.

Dietrich gave a toothy smile when Andy was in earshot, "Oh Andy, let me ride one of those horses for I cannot walk any farther."

"You are the very man I came after!" Andy said as he stiffly swung off his saddle.

Dietrich responded by lavishing praise on him, "There are few like you Andy! Few men would brave the wilds and with hostile Indians about! What a good boy you are indeed!" He capped his extolment of Andy's beneficence by adding, "I cannot go farther on my own because I was hiding in the water for eight hours!

Andy drew his lips into a smile, "I think you need to come down about four or five hours, friend."

"All right," he said with a broadening smile, "but indeed it seemed that long to me."

Andy dismounted and hooked his arm under the man's shoulders. He helped him over to a nearby log where he had positioned the spare horse. Taking the man's hand he guided him into the saddle and then adjusted the stirrups. They rode back to the hotel exchanging stories of what they had been through in the past 24 hours.

When they arrived at the hotel others came to greet them but Dietrich was too stiff get off his horse without help. A few men lifted him out of the saddle but after being helped off he was unable to walk; his legs were locking in a bent position. He lay on the ground rubbing life back into them as Andy led the horses away.

He turned Toby out to graze and then went back to his sunny patch of grass. He did not attempt to sleep, knowing it was futile. He was waiting for the others from his group to make it to the hotel. He could not tell the passage of time very well. It seemed to drag on endlessly. He waited until noon but no one else arrived at the hotel. A thought kept running through his head, "What if they were lying on the trail out there too weary to make the last few miles, like Dietrich?"

Now he was too anxious to wait. He went and saddled Toby once more, apologizing again. He rode down the trail at a lively pace for about eight miles. Coming to the crest of a small rise he reigned Toby to a stop. From his saddle he commanded a view that stretched another four miles down the trail. He pulled the looking glass from his saddlebag and put it to his eye. Sweeping the trail the entire four miles a few times he determined that no one was there. He had not heard any sign of them either.

He felt a sadness descend upon him. If they were okay they should have been this far by now. What had become of his friends? Sitting there on Toby would not provide the answer. Maybe they came to the hotel from another route and arrived during his absence? He determined to return to McCartney's and see if the others had arrived. If not, tomorrow he would better provision himself to go and look for them, all the way back to their final camp if he needed to! Perhaps he could even convince others to accompany him and make the job easier.

August 28th

Mammoth Hot Springs, Yellowstone Park

It was a beautiful day. The sun had risen brightly into a cloudless blue sky. The forest was filled with chatter from the forest creatures and the melody of songbirds floated across the prairie.

The day before, Andy had made known his intention to return to the camp. He approached every able-bodied man around the hotel to solicit their company on the trip. Each of them had reasons of why they were headed to Bozeman and could not help.

One of the men who owned an interest in the hotel, Jim McCartney, had been observing Andy. The man was taller than most but with an average build. The skin of his face and hands were brown and wrinkled by countless days in the sun and wind. At the corners of his eyes long lines fanned out and down his cheeks. The man either smiled or squinted a lot and Andy knew it was the later.

Even the manner of the man's dress cried out, "Frontiersman!" There was nothing superfluous on his clothing. The large scarf at his neck was tied for function only. His boots had the wear and tear only acquired from long and frequent use.

Andy watched as McCartney approached him and asked, "No luck?"

"No. Every man seems to have a prior engagement," Any replied without effort to disguise his disappointment. "I guess I will start out next evening alone and travel all night."

Jim, whom everyone called 'Mack', had lived on the frontier for long time. He took a long look at Andy, like he was sizing the man up. "If you can wait until the next morning I will go with you."

Andy considered the offer as the man continued to look him in the eye. He thought he had waited too long already. But…the idea of traveling alone did not sit well with him so he flashed a smile saying, "Thanks Mack, I would happy to have the company. I will be seeing you in the morning!" Andy had gone to bed with a much calmer mind than he thought he would a few hours earlier.

Now, McCartney and Andy had eaten breakfast and then finished preparations to return to the camp on Otter Creek. Each man had a saddle and a packhorse for the trip. Andy checked his tack one more time then swung into his saddle.

He looked down at Dietrich and said as a reminder, "You said you'd go in the ambulance with Stewart to Bozeman. You will care for him on the trip."

They had argued about that the day before. The German-born music teacher had smiled, shook his head, and replied in his thick German accent, "My God! What will Mrs. Roberts say if I go away and leave Joe? Through my inducement he came. What shall I say when I meet his mother, when she asks me, 'Where is Joe?'"

Andy had pursed his lips and shook his head. They had gone round and round about it since his return last night. It made no sense for Dietrich to stay because Andy and McCartney were going to go looking for the boys after they buried Kenck. He saw no reason for both of them to risk another Indian encounter on the slim chance the boys were still alive; it was taunting death!

Dietrich had finally capitulated but this morning something in his manner of speech made Andy feel that he did not intend on following through with it.

He shrugged; each man must make his own decision! Waving a goodbye to Stewart, he nodded to McCartney and the men turned their horses up the trail.

McCartney shouted over his shoulder to Dietrich, "Look out for your hair!"

Dietrich shouted back, "Andy, you will give me a decent burial, won't you?"

"You know I would!" Andy jested back and he heeled Toby forward shouting to McCartney, "Let's go Mack!"

They trotted down the trail and he calculated in his mind how far they could make it that day. If they pushed hard he figured they could make it to the old camp at dusk.

The men did ride hard, pushing their horses as fast as they could while ensuring their horses always had enough spare energy to flee from a war party if they crossed paths. It was a pleasant fall day and Andy enjoyed the crisp mountain air. He didn't say much to McCartney and the other man seemed to be of the same mind; they wanted to focus on their surroundings because the threat of an attack dominated their thoughts.

When they had a brief pause for lunch he answered McCartney's questions about where they had camped, where he had found Stone and Stewart, and what had been left at the camp. Andy respected the man's line of questioning. It was good information for McCartney to have if they had a run-in with Indians. With the short meal finished and the questions answered they mounted back up and again pushed hard for the old camp.

They saw no sign of Indians the entire day and late in the afternoon they had traveled to within a couple miles of the old camp. Andy calculated the distance and looked at the sun. He looked at McCartney who was having the same thoughts; they wouldn't make it by dark and should find a place to camp.

"We cannot make it today." Andy stated to open the conversation.

"I know. We would make it after dark, which is no good. I know of a fair camping spot just over that rise," McCartney flatly stated while pointing, "Let's set up camp and finish the trip in the morning when it will be light."

After the brief discussion they did just that. Traveling a short distance further they topped the rise and dropped down the other side. They arrived at small copse of trees near the creek and set up camp.

August 29th

Otter Creek, Yellowstone Park

The hair on nape of Andy's neck rose as they approached the old campsite. His senses were on heightened alert. They figured no Indians would be there but needed to be certain. They stopped to listen to the forest chatter and determined it was normal; likely no one was at the campsite. He urged his mount forward and McCartney followed his lead.

It was early morning and the dew clung to the grasses and brush leaves in heavy droplets. The horses were soaked to their hocks and the forest smelt of damp earth, pine, and sage.

Once in the glade the spectacle of chaotic scene was on full display. McCartney uttered a curse and Andy tried to harness the emotions broiling inside.

"I think that's where Stewart described Kenck's death cry having come from," Andy said pointing. McCartney followed his lead and they did a quick search but did not see a body.

"We should make ever-widening circles. You ride that way and I'll go in the opposite direction. But always keep me in sight," McCartney instructed.

Andy nodded and then turned his horse to search his area. Try as he did, Andy found it was impossible to maintain focus on the ground. His eyes kept wandering to the surrounding areas that could conceal Indians. Andy searched for only a few minutes before he spotted the back of Kenck's coat in the underbrush. "He's over here," Andy hollered to McCartney and rode over to his dead friend.

Saying a silent prayer for the man he dismounted and inspected the body. The back of his neck was a mangled mess and a large spot of dried blood overlapped on the center of his back. As far as Andy could tell Kenck had been shot in the back twice.

He rolled the body over to make certain it was Kenck. He looked down and his friend's face and into the empty eyes. Reaching down, Andy forcefully closed the eyelids. The man's full Vandyke and moustache were devoid of blood. Mercifully, the bullet in the neck had broken it, likely killing him instantly. If the back shot had come first then Andy would have found dried blood from the remains of lung froth as he gasped his last breaths.

His friend's pants and jacket pockets were turned inside out; obviously the Indians had looted him. Andy decided to search him anyway. He was surprised to feel the hard round shape in the man's vest breast pocket. Pushing his fingers into the pocket he found what he had expected; it still contained Kenck's pocket watch.

McCartney had arrived by then too. He saw Andy retrieving the watch and said, "Look, he still has a ring on his finger also. The Indians must have been in a real hurry!"

Andy worked at twisting the ring from his friend's finger. McCartney retrieved a shovel and a pickax from the packhorse and handed the latter to Andy. "There appears to be deep enough," the frontiersman said pointing at space of ground nearby.

The soil looked deep enough to prevent scavengers from ravaging Kenck's corpse. Andy grunted in affirmation and stepped over to Toby. He pulled a pair of cowhide work gloves from the saddlebag and shoved his hands into them. He was angry and cared not to control it.

Andy lifted the pickaxe overhead and brought it down with a giant heave. He poured his anger into physical work and ravaged the ground with such rapidity that it even surprised himself. It almost felt like he was exacting vengeance with each blow. McCartney was wise enough to keep silent and let him pour his grief into the work.

As Andy broke the earth with the pickax it allowed McCartney to follow up with the shovel. He was careful to stay clear of Andy's swings while shoveling the clods and loose dirt to the side. It wasn't until Andy was knee deep in the ground that he stopped for a breather.

"I think that's the best we can do," he said between gasps of air.

"I'm satisfied that the varmints won't disturb him," McCartney agreed, "Let's put him in and go hunting for those two boys."

Andy hooked his arms under Kenck's arms and McCartney grabbed under his knees. The carried the body to the grave and lowered it in as gently as they could. Andy stepped down in and doffed his hat. Wiping the rolling sweat from his brow he said, "I'll be back and give you a decent burial."

He then positioned the body to look at rest and stepped out. He pushed soil over the edge of the grave while McCartney shoveled it in. His friend slowly disappeared from view, the soil gradually covering him.

Andy piled a few large logs and rock on top the mound of dirt before taking off the gloves and saying, "Let's go find those boys."

They spent the rest of the day looking for Foller and Roberts, the young men of the group. They started by making the circular pattern that successfully had located Kenck. The hoof and foot prints were everywhere and neither of the could find anything definitively the boys. Their intense investigation uncovered no sign of them.

When one of their circles brought them near each other McCartney flagged him and shouted, "I don't think we'll find them this way. There is too much ground sign to know who was who."

Andy rode over to him, "I know. Let's return to the old camp and see if there is anything to be salvaged."

They turned their horses towards the remains of the camp. It didn't take long to pick through it. Andy was able to find a few pieces of cookware and cordage to keep. The rest of it was torn, broken, ripped, or burned. He put what he found into the packhorse's panyards and secured the straps down.

The darkening of dusk had yet to begin when Andy rode back into the previous night's campsite. Neither of them were up for talking. It had been a long and strenuous day. They set up the tent in the same place as before with no more than a few words between them.

Once it was up Andy said, "I'll go get wood and the start the fire." He stepped into the grove around them and searched for good kindling. He could hear McCartney preparing the supper while he finished getting what he needed. He returned with his arms full of wood and stooped down to start the fire. The light and warmth was calming and Andy felt some of the tension leave him.

They had their supper in silence, each lost in their own thoughts. Once he finished with the food Andy went and made his bed. Then they took their horse's halters and headed to a small cove of the meadow. Andy suggested, "Let's picket the horses tonight so they do not wander too far off."

McCartney stopped in his tracks. "Andy, something tells me we had better go on."

Andy studied the old frontiersman's face and after a short pause replied, "Alright Mack, let's saddle up."

Andy took Toby back to the camp and packed his bedding again. He swung into the saddle and settled himself as McCartney finished securing his bedding. They started to skirt the meadow, hugging the timberline.

They had been riding for a few moments when Andy stole a glance back at their camp through an opening in the timber. There riding across the meadow was an Indian warrior bearing down on them!

"Indian!" Andy hissed as he heeled Toby to full speed.

McCartney was right on Toby's tail and they lit out of there. They ran the horses until they were winded and then trotted them until they were slick with sweat. Andy pulled out his watch and checked the time; it was 3 o'clock in the morning.

"Have you seen any other Indians," he asked as McCartney pulled next to him.

"Not since that one," he replied while wiping his brow. "Let's camp after crossing the Yellowstone," Andy suggested, "I reckon there isn't far to go to the hotel but I'm knackered and my horses are completely exhausted. I think we need to stop for the night."

"I know a good crossing down here," McCartney said leading the way down the hillside.

Andy trailed him to a shallow crossing where the river broadened and the riffles of water flowing over shallow rocks extended nearly the entire width of the Yellowstone. He directed Toby into the water and splashed across in McCartney's breakers.

At the other side they rode until McCartney found a well-concealed and defensible campsite. The willows stretched for over ten feet tall and the only point of entry was easily observed for over 100 yards. Anyone who saw them would need to come from that direction and had little cover. Andy felt it was an easy place to fend off an attack if it happened. They reined their horses over and again made their beds. Afterwards they hobbled the horses so they could get enough food. The poor animals had been pushed hard the past few days.

Both men quickly were sound asleep. Andy woke first. They had decided the night before to get an early start and he intended to do just that. Rolling out of his bedding he stomped into his boots, grabbed his gun, and went to get the horses.

They were nowhere to be seen! He reflexively tightened the grip on his gun. Perhaps they went out from the willows he thought. He cautiously walked down to the end of the willows. No horses were in sight. His heart jumped in his throat and his entire body was on full alert. Andy looked around; perhaps Indians had stolen the horses!

"Mack! Our horses are gone," He called to McCartney. It was but a few moments before the man was next to him.

"Let's mount a search. You go that way and I'll go this way," he instructed, "if we don't find them in a mile or so let's meet back here."

"With Indians about I'd feel better if we stayed together, Mac."

"I recon your right. That'd be wise. Let's start this way," he conceded.

They went down one direction a ways and looked across the hills and into the small folds of land for nearly an hour without any sign of them. Then they turned back and searched the other direction in similar fashion and with similar results.

Andy was concerned and wondered aloud, "Perhaps they had been stolen during the night."

"I don't know that they would stop with just the horses," he replied as he crested a small rise.

Then McCartney hollered, "I had found them!"

Andy sighed with relief and hurried over. There they were happily eating grass without a care in the world. Toby lifted his head to look over then reached back down and ripped out another mouthful of lush green grass.

The horses nickered at them and then Toby walked over to greet Andy. The men easily slipped the horses halters and ropes on and led them back to the camp. "It is shaping up to be another beautiful morning," Andy said more to himself than McCartney.

As Andy tightened the final strap on his packhorse he pulled out his pocket watch; it was 9 o'clock in the morning. Camp was packed and they were on their way to the Springs again.

McCartney pulled up in an opening until Andy was next to him. He turned and said with a smile, "Now in the light of day, I realize that only 18 miles separate us from my hotel. We will be there by dinner if we have no problems!"

Andy could feel his mood improve with each mile closer they drew to the relative safety of the hotel and the other men. The sun felt warmer on his face. The birds seemed more numerous and all in song. The blue of the sky and green of the grass seemed more vibrant. He stole a look over at McCartney and could tell he felt the same when the man looked over at him and flashed a rare grin.

They had been traveling for less than half an hour when they rounded a bend of a small hill. Down the trail was something that instantly changed their moods. A band of Indian warriors were riding the up trail towards them! Andy quickly calculated 18 of them and that they were within 200 yards of each other. He could make out the Indians' faces and they looked just as surprised as Andy felt!

"Strike for the brush!" Andy yelled as he quirted Toby towards the nearest brush, about a mile distant.

The war party tried to intercept them before they made good their escape into the brush. It was a lively race for that entire mile. The Indians' war whoops and the bellows of their rifles shattered the mountain silence. The 18 Indian guns plus the pair from Andy and McCartney maintained quite a racket, filling the plain with constant gunfire.

Andy heard a bullet whistling past and saw it kick up dust a dozen yards in front of him. Then another zipped past close enough to make him hug closer to Toby and he saw the dust kicked up a few yards in front of him! He looked at McCartney who also ducked lower on his horse's neck. The Indians were zeroing in on them! As McCartney started to steer his horse straight up the steep hill towards the brush, Andy decided to keep out on the hillside more. He wanted to give his horse a better chance to make their escape.

Despite his choice, Toby labored to climb the hill at the speed with which he had crossed the prairie. Andy stole a glance over his shoulder and saw that their pursuers were in various stages of dismounting and getting cover behind a reef of rocks at the base of the hill. They were still a good 200 yards away. The assailants continued to pour lead at the two men and dust was kicking up all around Andy on the hillside.

Suddenly Toby came to a dead stop, almost pitching Andy over its neck. He knew something was seriously wrong and jumped from the saddle and instantly saw blood running out of Toby's side.

He looked for targets down at the reef of rocks. Here and there heads would bob in and out of sight; he could not see enough of the Indians behind the rocks to shoot at them! He also did not have enough cartridges to waste on low-probability shots.

"Goodbye Toby, I have not time to stay, but must make the rest of the way afoot." He said stroking the horse's forehead once before bolting for the brush.

Running up the hill he could see McCartney ahead on his horse, bullets kicking up dust around him too. Suddenly the saddle slipped back onto the horse's rump and it bucked and kicked out with its hind legs. McCartney flew from the saddle, landing hard on his side with a loud grunt. The horse ran right over towards Andy, the saddle now hanging below it over its belly.

As he ran Andy pulled his knife from its sheath thinking, "If the horse came close enough, I could grab the reigns and cut the saddle loose. Then I'd and ride it bareback."

Unfortunately during the few seconds he thought this, the wild-eyed horse bucked, kicked, and trampled the saddle until it came off. It then changed course and lit out away from him. So much for the ride!

The entire time bullets were whizzing towards and past him, kicking up dust all around him. McCartney was running towards him and Andy changed course to meet the man. While running and dodging his way to McCartney, he saw Toby keel over.

"They must have shot at least 50 times by now!" He thought aloud as the men met in the middle. Andy noticed a bullet had cut a piece from his bootleg but the barrage had hit neither him nor McCartney!

"Lets get down behind that log!" McCartney shouted between gasping for air and pointing to a big log lying close by.

Andy looked up and saw Indians making their way above them. He shook his head, "I am going for the brush!"

"Wait for me to take off my spurs, I will go with you!" McCartney said putting his hand on Andy's shoulder while yanking off the spurs with the other hand.

As the spurs came off, McCartney tossed them towards the log, "They can lay there until sometime later when I might call for them!" Three more shots had been fired at them during the doffing of the spurs, each bullet striking within ten feet of the men.

"The bullets are coming pretty thick!" Andy commented sourly.

"Just so." Retorted McCartney as they began the dash for the brush once more.

Soon they were pushing into the cover of the brush and the firing stopped. They kept driving through the brush for some distance before turning to check on their pursuers; they could neither see nor hear any sign of them.

"They are terribly brave so long as they have the advantage, but just as soon as the tables are turned they make themselves scarce!" Andy thought aloud while trying to catch his breath.

"Let's wait in the brush for a while," Suggested McCartney between his own gasps for air.

"I'm going to position myself over there," Andy stated pointing several rods away to an edge of the brush that was thick all the way to the openness beyond, "I will be able to see down the hill to the reef of rocks."

"I'm going there," McCartney point a few rods the other direction, "and cover our flanks."

The men separated and took up their positions. Andy saw some movement at the reef at first but then nothing. His heart was racing and the pounding in his ears drowned out all other sounds. He calmed his heart and breathing.

Time drug on. There was no movement or sound from below, behind, or either side. The Indians seemed to have given up! Andy checked his pocket watch; they had waited for over an hour without sign of an Indian.

McCartney suggested hopefully, "Lets go see if the walking is good, or possibly they had missed one of our horses."

McCartney followed as Andy carefully ventured to the edge of their cover. Pushing the brush to the side with his off hand Andy eased forward. He was ready to dive back if they saw any movement. None came. He slowly straightened up, still ready to dive into the brush. Nothing stirred anywhere around the rock reef.

"I want to go see if they can find Toby," Andy said as McCartney straightened up next to him.

They started down the steep hillside in the direction they had come. Both men were ready to fight, guns at the ready if they were needed.

Andy could see Toby was dead long before they made it down to him. The horse's chest was not moving with any breathing. When they arrived at the body there was no saddle or bridle; the Indians had taken them both. Andy squatted down, put his hand on Toby's forehead, and said a silent goodbye.

Andy looked out across the plain as he stood back up. There in the distance was the group of mounted warriors riding. "Look there they are," he said pointing them out to McCartney.

"They are about four miles off and heading away," McCartney stated flatly after studying them, "We need to make it to the Springs on foot."

With that they began to walk. It felt good to Andy to be stretching his legs and moving after the being cramped up in the brush for a few hours. They kept up their vigilance for Indians but no signs of their enemy were seen.

They made good time for being afoot but it was getting towards dark when they finally came to the Gardiner River where McCartney had planned to cross. The water was flowing strong and fast. In the fading light it was hard for Andy to see the bottom.

"It looks pretty deep," Andy said with a little concern in his voice.

McCartney shook his head in agreement, "Looks less daunting from the back of a horses. Let's find a better place to cross."

They spent almost the entire next an hour walking down the river to find a suitable crossing. Finally they found a riffle to cross and McCartney said, "This will do. Let's strip down first."

Andy removed his clothing being careful to fold them into a tight a bundle that he could easily balance on the top his head while crossing. McCarntey had done the same and already was several feet into the water. Andy followed his path and waded into the water. It was freezing cold and the first step made him want to turn right around!

He forced his legs forward into the icy river and carefully continued to make his way across. As the ground angled down the waters hit his nether region and really took his breath away! He focused on his footing and resisting the force of the river as the water tried to push him downstream. If he lost his footing he would be in trouble!

Up ahead he could see McCartney now up to his chin in the water. He had one hand holding his rifle and the other to balance his clothing on the top of his head. Fortunately there was only a rod more until the far bank.

As Andy felt the water raising to his neck he held tighter to the gun and clothing. When McCartney reached the other side, Andy would have sighed in relief had any air been left in his lungs!

Gaining the other side, Andy followed McCartney's example. As he dripped off in the cold evening air he stepped over to a nearby leafy brush and plucked a handful of leaves from the branches. His shaking hands made this more difficult than he expected but soon he was wiping down with leaves from nearby brush. It was more wicking away the water than drying himself but it felt better.

With the moisture off they dressed. Andy pulled on his long underwear and pants, his freezing cold fingers fumbled with the buttons and he had an especially hard time with the belt. The worse of it was his wounded shoulder was stiff and painful. It throbbed and burned as he thread the arm into his shirt and pulled on his coat.

"I'll be back momentarily. I need to make my toilet," McCartney stated and walked upstream. Andy turned and went downstream to do the same business. Then they went separate ways and made their toilet.

When they met back at the river. Andy's stomach rumbled loudly. "I am getting awful hungry," he commented.

"We are only two miles from the Springs, we will get something to eat when we get to the house." McCartney consoled.

Darkness had fallen and they started a brisk walk to drive the chill away. It wasn't long before they could see the house.

It was expectedly dark inside. As they closed the distance Andy found it odd that no smoke came from the chimney either.

Their hopes for food and safety were dashed; as they drew even closer to the building they made out that the front door was standing open.

"They might mistake us for Indians," McCartney said before he called out, "Hello boys! We have returned. Its Mack and Andy; don't shot!"

There was no answer from the house. They looked at each other and Andy shrugged concomitantly.

They stepped into the building. McCartney led them to a corner of the room and retrieved something. Andy heard the strike of a match and saw McCartney hold the flame to the wick of a candle lying on a table. As the candle's light brightened the room they turned around at the same time. In that same moment Andy saw poor Dietrich lying dead on the floor.[vii]

Andy bent down on a knee to examine his friend. He had been shot three times. There were two shots in the chest; one had pierced his heart, killing him instantly. The third shot had entered the crown of his head and travelled through the length of his body before exiting through the pelvis. It must have been delivered after he fell.

"The others must be somewhere around here dead too, we should find them." Andy solemnly stated.

They made an armed search of the house but found no one else. Then they expanded their search into the outbuildings and still found no one else. So, they expanded their search again to include out into yard. That search yielded the same lack of results. "There aren't anymore dead here," McCartney state, "let's return to the house."

About this time Andy's shoulder began throbbing so badly it reached a new level of pain. He was in agony. His mind thought back over the past week. He had passed through so much in that time and with no more than three to four hours of sleep! The last time he had been at the hotel ee had been unable to sleep for worry about the missing boys. Now he felt his body was shutting down, almost giving out. He sat down while McCartney hunted around the house again, this time for some food.

He returned empty-handed. There was nothing left; the Indians had taken every bit of it. "We should go down the river to the next ranch; it is only seven miles away. They would have food as well as be a safe place to sleep," McCartney said less as a statement than an imperative.

Andy felt like camping anywhere, here sounded as good to him as the next ranch. He was hurting and was exhausted, all he wanted was to lie down and sleep. But, to satisfy McCartney he agreed to make the trek. They set out immediately with McCartney in the lead and Andy moseying behind.

111

When they arrived at the road McCartney stopped him. Looking at it in the moonlight he pointed, " There are too many fresh horse-tracks going the same direction we are. There must be more Indians ahead, keep a good lookout." They checked their guns before starting off again.

Whenever they saw something move or heard a noise, they would hurry over to the sagebrush on the side of the road. It made for slow going but was necessary. It also kept Andy attentive and his mounting fatigue at bay. Occasionally they could hear someone just ahead of them on the road. Each time they heard the noise they darted to the brush. After several near meetings they decided to keep off the road until the moon fully rose. They had not made it far like this when Andy became too tired to continue.

He apologized to McCartney, "I need to sleep about an hour, then wake me." Then he flopped down behind a large sagebrush. He was fast asleep before his head touched the ground.

Andy woke to McCartney whispering for him to wake up. He slowly set his mind in motion and finally pushed through the cobwebs that dulled his mind. McCartney's face slowly came into focus.

It was still dark outside but he could tell that more than an hour had passed since he lay down. He was grateful, now he felt he could keep traveling. They furtively moved to the road and listened; nothing could be heard and they crept towards the ranch.

It had been less than half an hour when Andy could make out the silhouette of the ranch house in the distance. Suddenly a bell clanged and both men froze. It rang again and they relaxed.

"Sounds like a cow," Andy stated softly.

"At least we will have some milk if nothing else," McCartney jested.

Suddenly a man stood up from the sagebrush in front of them. They were so surprised that they froze for a split second before dropping to their knees and shouldering their rifles. Andy's finger was tightening on his trigger when the man called out, "Who comes there?"

He recognized the voice of a white man just in time to save him. His finger eased off the trigger as he stood up with McCarthy at his side. "Friends," they answered in unison.

"Come on in then," The man answered and waved them over. They now noticed that he wore a soldier's uniform as he ushered them to a camp. It then dawned on Andy that was the cause of all the horse tracks on the road; it had been the cavalry!

As they entered the rows of soldiers' tents, the guard said, "It has been a busy night. A negro man just came in a little time before you."

"Ben? Was his name Ben Stone," Andy asked with excitement.

The man shrugged noncommittally. Suddenly a man behind the guard jumped up from the ground and ran to Andy; he recognized it was Ben before the man spoke.

Taking Andy's hand and shaking it with vigor he nearly shouted, "God bess you Andy! I neber expectin' to seed you no moah!" Ben's face flowed freely with tears and he choked-up, unable to speak anymore.

The guard led them to the officer in charge of the company, Lieutenant Doane. He was a towering man of 6'2" height with a lean 200-pound physique. Sporting a wax-sharpened moustache that extended past the side of his face even at this hour, the blue-eyed officer was intimidating. He asked a few questions then dismissed the men after they answered.

Andy lay down, but once again sleep eluded him. Not only had he just taken a long nap but also Ben and he could not stop talking. Andy relayed what he and Wilkie had gone through again and answered any questions Ben had. Then he told of his adventure with McCartney and answered another slough of questions.

Then it was Ben's turn to explain. He retold what had happened after Andy and Wilkie had left; how the camp was attacked and what he did to escape. Andy had a few questions and then Ben continued with what transpired after he and McCartney left the Springs.

"I seed de Injuns comin' aroun' in the foah-noon dis mornin'. I tole Detrcih we had better be a getting' out of dis, but he kept a saying' 'I'll neber go back to Mrs. Roberts widout Joe.' "Bout 'leven or twelve o'clock Detrich says, 'I'll go down and change de hosses, repicket dem, while you git dinnah, Ben.' I say 'all right.'

"Well, while he was gone a changin' ob de hosses, I looked out ob de doah an' seed a Injun stick his head up ober a rock out in front ob de house. I didn't wait for no lebe, I didn't, an' dropped eberyting an' bolted trew de back doah, I did, up into de timbah an' laid down awaiting' for somethin' to do next. I seed de Injun's all 'bout de house an' pears like dey mighty anxious to fine me, but I wasen't anxious to fine dem. It war getting along towards night, and I clim a tree. Purty soon a big injun rode right down under de tree a searchin' for me. I jes hel' my bref an' say to myself, 'Oh Mr. Injun; good Mr. Injun, don't look up dis way!" Boys, I 'clare to goodness I could hab touched dat Injun's head wif my foot—*but I didn't!*

"Bye'm-bye de Injun go away down towards de springs an' I got down on to de ground an' strike for de side ob de mountain whar I laid down. I was a layin' in the brush, when all ob a sudden I heerd a crackin in de brush. Den, boys, I got right down on my knees and prayed, (an' I hope de God Almighty forgive me, I neber prayed before sense I lef' my modder's knee), but I

115

jes got down an' say O' Lod God A'mighty, jes help me out dis scrape an' I will never interfere wid you no moah!' I heerd dis noise an' a crashin' in the bushes again, and I jes laid down wid my face to the ground' an I spected to feel de tom hawk in de back of my head. All ob a sudden I turned ober and dar I seed a big black bear lookin' at me. Boys, *I nebber was so glad to see a bar afore in all my life.* De bar he got up an' run, an' I got up an' rund to de top ob de mountain when I saw dis camp fire and heah I is—bress de Lod!"[viii]

Andy had more questions now that a story was being told that he had not heard. Finally, Ben satisfied his curiosity and continued on how he had entered the camp not long before Andy:

"When I had come up to the guard and he asked me, 'Who comes dar?'

'Ben Stone,' I said.

He then said, 'Come in Ben Stone.'

And you bet I came running! He had two Indian scouts with him. They jumped up and came with their hands out saying, 'How! How!' Then I went running cause I thought I got an Indian camp! The guard called me back, but I would not believe that the fellow who had the buckskin suit was not Chief Joseph and the others were not some of his tribe until you showed up Andy!"

Andy could barely keep his eyes open, he felt completely parched, and his head throbbed with each beat of his heart. He felt his head swaying on his neck and new that he had better find some water and try and rest. Looking over at his friend Andy stated, "Ben, it is good to see you made it through! I am about to die from over from lack of water and sleep; where can a man some water around here?"

Ben pointed, "Ober dar, Andy. You gits rested."

Andy filled his canteen and staggered back to his bedding. Ben was fast asleep. When Andy put his head down but his shoulder's throbbing pain prevented sleep. Then his mind perseverated on the boys he had not found. He kept playing the scene of him telling their mothers what happened and how he did not find them. It was pure anguish seeing their distraught faces and hearing their screams of lamentation.

August 30th

Mammoth Hot Springs, Yellowstone Park

Andy winced as his horse's heavy stepping sent shocks of pain shooting through his shoulder. The pain had grown worse over the past day despite the large scab that had formed. More taxing than the bullet wound was his sleep deprivation. His head throbbed and his vision was not as it should be; only having clarity in the center of where he looked. It reminded him of being drunk. His mind moved slowly and his reactions even slower. Everything was out of sync and he had to force his mind to focus.

He was in the lead of a large group of men. Tightly grouped behind him rode soldiers and citizens, all looking to the edges of the timber searching for signs of Indians. The group was traveling to McCartney's Hotel to bury Dietrich. There was not much talking; everyone was still being vigilant about looking for an ambush. Ben rode next to Andy, both lost in their own thoughts.

When they arrived at the hotel, he and Ben went to the body first. The other men stayed in the yard and gave them privacy. The pair needed to say their goodbyes to their compatriot.

Andy walked over to the corpse and stood looking at his friend's face. He said, "He was a good friend. He had a quick wit and will be sorely missed."

Ben then choked out between his tears, "I neber knowah moah genteel man."

Then they set about straightening up the man's clothing. Andy finished by telling Dietrich, "I'll keep my promise to you, Dick."

Meanwhile McCartney took the rest of the men and went in search of wood for a coffin. After a short while they came back with a meager supply, not even enough to construct a full coffin. Lumber was scarce but they all agreed that what they had found would not do. McCartney remembered that he had an old wooden bathtub that he decommissioned not long ago due leaks too numerous to patch. It was obvious to everyone that the only option was to bury Dietrich in the bathtub.

Andy and Ben went in search of a gravesite. They had not walked far when they found a suitable place; on the other side of Clematis Creek an earthy spot that looked deep enough to inter the body. They buried the body and said a few words over it. The crowd disbursed and went their separate ways. Andy was already focused on his next task; finding the two lost boys.

He strode back to McCartney's hotel to pack the things for departure. When he finished, he found McCartney waiting for him outside the front door. Andy shook McCartney's hand and thanked him for all the help. They shared the bond that only men who faced death together and survived have.

The man returned his handshake with vigor and asked what he planned now. Andy replied, "I am heading back to Bozeman. I need to replenish my wardrobe and get supplies. I also will need a couple of horses because I am going looking for the boys. And I intend to look until I find them."

"I'm sure you will, Andy. Good luck!"

With that, Andy swung onto his borrowed horse and headed off. He traveled the balance of the day and was within five miles of Bozeman when he met another traveler on the road. The men stopped to talk and when the traveler discovered Andy's identity and mission, he smiled. He told Andy that the boys had walked into Virginia City about three days earlier. He figured that they had made it to Helena by then.

Andy could not contain his joy! In fact, he did not even try to contain it; he gave three loud cheers and thanked the man. Heeling his borrowed horse in the ribs he went flying down the canyon at full speed. When he made it to town, he headed straight for the town gossips and got all the particulars.

The boys, Roberts and Foller, took the direction of Virginia City as near as they could guess. They made it in three days walking and on only eating a single small fish each and some berries![ix]

Andy's ordeal was now finished. He could relax and get some rest. The first thing that he did was crawl into a bed and fall fast asleep.

Appendix
Helena Party Accounts

Lakochets Kunnin (Rattle Blanket) led the Nez Perce war party to find the tourists. Without warning, several warriors assaulted the camp by running into it and firing their rifles. The attack was quick and the tourists were completely surprised. They scattered like a covey of quail, running in all directions with the warriors in hot pursuit.

Duncan, already more on edge than the others, sprang up like a deer and fled before the others realized what was happening. But, the others were not long in following suit. Frederic Pfister was in the edge of the forest collecting firewood and at the first shot turned and sprinted towards the Yellowstone River, hurdling Otter Creek along the way. Richard Dietrich fled in the same direction but was unable to clear Otter Creek when he attempted to jump across it. With a huge splash he instead landed in it. He decided to remain in the water as the Nez Perce pursuers passed by him. He stayed partially submerged for several hours, listening while the Nez Perce plundered the camp.

Leander Duncan had also stayed in the woods to hide. Finding the thickest part of the forest he forced himself deep into it and waited. After night fell and the darkness set in he started to Mammoth Hot Springs.

John Stewart and Charles Kenck sprinted off together. The warriors' bullets struck Stewart in the leg and hip and he fell hoping the Indians would pass by him. They did, chasing Kenck until they caught up with him. They shot him twice; once in the back and the other breaking his neck. Stewart heard Kenck cry out, "Oh my God!" and then there was silence.

Not long after Kenck's final cry, a warrior came back to Stewart and demanded money. Stewart was turned over and his pockets rifled through; they took $263 and his silver watch. After his robbers left, Stewart made a failed attempt to find Kenck or any others of the party. He gave up the pursuit and limped back to the camp since the warriors had left by then.

The camp was in disarray. The Indians had splintered the shotguns across trees and tossed anything they did not want on the campfire. The ground was strewn with random items. He found an overcoat that he put on and then soaked his hip wound in the stream. While soaking he decided that the Mammoth Hot Springs, although a difficult hike, would be the most likely rendezvous point. He set out on what he expected to be a long hike to Mammoth Hot Springs. He had not gone far before his mare noticed him and walked up to him. He led her to a log to mount and once in the saddle started off again. The pain in his leg and the lack of balance owing to being bareback made it harder to ride than walk so he slide off and lead his horse. He came to Cascade Creek where he washed his wounds again before continuing on. He traveled about a mile when he chanced upon Ben Stone. When the shooting had begun, Stone had run away down the hill but tripped and somersaulted to the bottom where he landed in the stream. He hid there for three hours while the warriors plundered the camp.

"Are you wounded?," asked Stewart.

"No I am not," replied the cook.

Stewart nodded to his leg, "I'm shot it in the leg and hip but whether badly or not I cannot tell." Ben looked at his leg and Stewart added, " Will you stay with me and help me through to the Springs?"

Without hesitation Ben said, "Yes sir, I will." The two of them sat down together and split what little food they had. They ate the meager lunch and once finished started down the trail.

On the 30th an ambulance crewman, Jake Stoner, spotted a party of Indians. He was hunting when he saw them near Lava Creek. He rushed back to McCartney's and warned Dietrich and Ben Stone. Both men fled to hide in the brush. The warriors appeared a little later and searched the buildings and the around them.

Stone narrowly missed the approaching Nez Perce as he fled up a gulch to a timbered point of rocks behind the buildings.

The warriors left riding North towards Henderson's ranch, 6 miles from Mammoth Springs and along the wagon road to Bozeman. James Henderson had established it just outside the Park boundary in 1871 and now was managed by his son, Sterling. Sterling provided mining supplies and mail services to the local prospectors.

On August 31 Sterling and John Werks were at the ranch house when at mile's distance they noticed the war party of 18 heading their direction. The two men quickly gathered up weapons and ammunition belts before racing to the Yellowstone River 300 yards to the east. Three men were fishing at the river, Joseph Brown, George Reese, and William Davis. The five men quickly set up a strong defensive position among boulders 100 yards from the house. They watched as the war party broke into two groups: a group of ten stopped and watched as the remaining eight continued their advance to the ranch.

When the warriors went to the corrals to steal the horses the five men in the boulders unleashed a fusillade at them. The sudden and thunderous gun reports and whizzing bullets spooked the Nez Perce horses off. The eight mountless warriors ran to cover behind the house and barn, returning fire as they secured safe positions.

After over two hours of shooting the ranchers decided to withdraw. They would retreat to the river and cross in the boat moored there. They made a dash for the boat and the ten mounted warriors and sent bullets at them as they rowed for the other side. The other eight warriors had set the buildings on fire and dark black smoke belched from all the structures. Then they gathered their horses and those from the corral and all 18 raced away towards Mammoth Springs. Not long after the warriors disappeared over the horizon a large contingent of cavalry arrived from the direction of Cinnabar Mountain. The force was led by Lieutenant Gustavus C. Doane. He was reconnoitering with Company E 7th Cavalry, 42 Crow scouts, and a handful of wagons when he saw the plume of smoke rising in the sky.

Dietrich thought the danger had passed and returned to McCartney's for food. As he stood in the doorway of the log hotel, *Chuslum Hahlap Kanoot* (Naked-footed Bull) decided to kill the music teacher from Helena. The warrior had lost many family members at the Big Hole battle and was enraged. He shot Dietrich in the heart and then again when the man staggered out to the front porch plunging face-first into the dirt. The third and final shot entered the crown of his head and traveled the length of his body.

Not long afterwards ten men under Doane's command guided by local mountain man Collins J. "Jack" Barronett arrived at the hotel and found Dietrich's body still warm. They drug his corpse back onto the hotel floor.

The small detachment traveled by Liberty Cap geyser and gave chase to the warriors until Lava Creek. Barronett insisted that they break off the pursuit and return to Doane's bivouac at Henderson's Ranch. Second Lieutenant Hugh L. Scott agreed this was wise and they turned back.

"Our party consisted of Kenk, Stuart, Roberts, Foller, Weikart, Duncan, Detrich, Wilkie, Ben Stone, the colored cook, and myself, and were on our way to visit the Geyser Basins. Yesterday we were encamped near Sulphur Mountain, and during the afternoon one of the boys said he had seen either a herd of buffalo or elk, or a band of Indians, about five or six miles above us on the other side of the Yellowstone river. Duncan took a spyglass and went up on the mountain to determine if possible, what they were. He soon returned and said they were Indians, and proposed that we get out of there as soon as possible. We accordingly packed up and moved back three or four miles, when one of the boys proposed that we go no farther, as Howard was after the Indians, and by tomorrow they would be gone, and we pitched our tents there. We camped for the night, but some of the boys wanted to go back home. The majority was of the mind to go ahead to the geysers, as we had come this far, and the journey was almost completed."

Frederic Pfister, Helena Party

"We were just on the point of leaving the Sulphur Springs, when Duncan came running down from the top of Sulphur Mountain, exclaiming, 'There's a damn big party of tourists, or else a big band of elk, ahead!' Wilkie said, 'Yes, your elk will turn out to be trees, like all the rest of the game you see.' After traveling three or four miles the boys began to grow uneasy. We could see something alive coming, but did not know what it was. We traveled on and, on reaching the top of a small hill, saw a large camp across the Yellowstone. Duncan exclaimed, 'Indians! Indians! My God, it's Indians!' He wanted us to backtrack. We traveled back at a very lively rate for five or six miles to Sulphur Springs, where our scare seemed to subside a little when we found a beautiful and safe camp."

"We finally agreed to wait until the next day when two of us would go and ascertain if the camp had moved, and if so, which way, and etc. We then went to bed. Duncan, not feeling safe, took his blankets and made his bed half a mile from camp in the timber, all of us laughing at him."

Ben Stone, Helena Party. September 6, 1877

"I know one that did not close his eyes, and that was your humble servant. I felt as though someone ought to stay awake; if the truth was known, I felt pretty nervous."

Andrew Weikert, Helena Party

"We got up about six or seven o'clock this morning, and Andy Weikart and Wilkie took their horses and went out on a scout. They were to fire their guns if they saw Indians, and we waited three or four hours for them to return. It was nearing dinnertime and I left the camp for the purpose of getting wood, leaving some of the boys asleep, and the remainder sitting about the campfire. I was busy getting wood when all of a sudden, pop, pop, pop, went the guns and I heard the Indians' yip! yip! I looked around and saw the camp full of Indians with the boys jumping and going in every direction. I saw two of the boys coming towards me and I lit out for the river. I reached the river and on looking back heard two shots and someone exclaim, 'Oh my God!' I don't know who these two people were but I think it was Jack Stuart and Kenk."

Frederic Pfister, Helena Party

"That same day [when Weikert and McCartney left to bury Kenck] 18 or 20 Indians came down the river. A man by the name of Stoner, who used to live near Tiffin, was out around the

Springs hunting when he saw a couple of parties coming across the prairie. He thought they were Indians, so he went to the house, saddled his horse and told Stone that a couple of parties were coming up from the river. Stone said, "That is Andy with the boys, so I will be getting them something to eat." But Stoner said no, he thought they were Indians. Just at this time they made their appearance, so Stoner mounted his horse and went out where Dietrich was re-picketing a horse. He was about a mile from the house. Stoner told him to take to the brush for there were Indians at the Springs. So he must have made good his escape until the next day about noon, when he must have come back to the house while the Indians had gone down the river on a horse-stealing excursion. I presume he came back to get something to eat at the house, when the Indians returned with about 20 head of horses they had captured and the soldiers headed them off so they had to return. When they got to the Springs Dietrich was there and they shot him down like a dog; put 3 bullets through him, one entering his heart. He was lying just off the steps when the soldiers came up, and his body was still warm. They carried him into the house and left him there until the next day, then they followed the Indians farther. Stone made good his escape from the tree where Ben was and stopped under it. Old Ben said his heart beat so loud and fast that he was afraid that the Indianskin would hear it beat, but it seems that he did not for he soon rode off up the gulch. Ben hugged the tree close and stayed there until after dark when he slipped down and crawled over a hill where he again ventured out. Ben said, "Five times I started out of dem brush and five times I went back again, then I prayed fervently to Almighty God to deliver me out of dis trouble and by God he did take me out." A bear came to see him while he was in the brush so he was undecided what to do. If he stayed there, the bear would be apt to eat him, and if he would run out of the brush, the Indians were likely to kill him, but he finally decided in favor of the bear because he had tried the Indians twice. When the bear saw him, it stood on its hind feet and looked at him for a while and then ran away.

Andrew Weikert, Helena Party

"Pfister and Detrich jumped over an embankment and started for the Yellowstone River. Pfister jumped the creek at or near the camp, but Detrich was not so fortunate but fell in, and it happened to be in a hole so he laid quite still. The grass was high on either side. He stayed in the water for about four hours. The Indians did not see him, so he made good his escape after they, the Indians, had left camp. Roberts and Foller did some tall running, according to their own account, while the

Indians were blazing away at them most every jump, but finally got away all safe. They struck out for Virginia City, which was about 150 miles. The first night they camped in the timber, they laid down beside a big log. One of the boys had a coat on and the other hadn't, so the one with the coat had to lay on the outside. They traveled the next day; they were getting pretty hungry, so they tried fishing. Caught two little fishes. They built a fire and roasted one; the other they saved for another meal. Those two fishes were all they had to eat for nearly three days. They met some soldiers in the afternoon of the third day; they got what they wanted to eat and got enough to last them to Virginia.

Duncan, he lit out from the camp like a scared wolf, and got where the timber was the thickest and stayed until dark. He then struck out for the Mammoth Springs. Stewart and Kenk did not fare so well. The Indians followed them up and shot Stewart in the side and in the calf of the leg. He fell. Then they followed Kenk up until they killed him. Shot him through the body; one ball struck him in the back of the neck and broke it. I suppose it killed him instantly. They raffled his pockets, then came back and was going to kill Stewart. He asked them to spare his life; they asked him if he had any money. They rolled him over and took 260 dollars and a silver watch. After a time they told him he could live. So they left him; he dragged himself down to the creek and washed his wound. He looked up and saw his mare coming toward him; he got a halter and put it on her and then he led her to a log and crawled onto her. He rode her about 1 mile, but his wound pained him so that he had to get off her. About this time Stone came hobbling along. He was afflicted with rheumatism anyway, and laying in the water so long had done him no good.

We helloed a couple times, but received no answer. Then rode into camp and found that the boys had got away in a hurry by the things that were laying around promiscuously. They, the boys, did not take time to take their outfits or anything except their clothes they had on their backs. The Indians did not want the shotguns, so they smashed them around the trees so as to make them unfit for further use. They took what they needed in shape of blankets, provisions, saddles and fourteen head of horses. What they did not want, they put on the fire and burned up. They gave the boys a complete surprise."

Andrew Weikert, Helena Party

"I turned my horse out to graze and waited until noon for the rest of the boys to come in, but none came. I then saddled my horse again and went back on the trail again about eight miles and from this point could see about four miles more, but could not see nor hear anything of them. I returned sad at heart but with a determination to go back and hunt for them if I could persuade someone to go with me. No one volunteered to go with me. So I concluded to start the next evening alone but Jim McCarty, who owned an interest in the Springs and has lived on the frontier a long time, told me if I would wait until the next morning, he would go with me. We started the next morning with two saddle horses and two packhorses leaving Detrich, Stewart, and Stone at the Springs. The ambulance was coming up after Stewart that day and I begged Detrich to go with him and take care of him, but he wanted to wait until I came back. When we started, Mack told him to look out for his horse; he said he would try to, adding, 'Andy, you will give me a decent burial, won't you?' I told him jestingly that I would, never thinking that I would be called on to perform the reality so soon."

McCartney and I found Charles Kenck's body at Otter Creek and buried him. Upon our return to Mammoth Hot Springs, we found Dietrich as well, lying dead in the hotel. Fearing that Ben Stone might be dead and Mammoth Hot Springs no longer a safe place, we made our way north into the safety of Lt. Doane's camp. There we found Ben Stone the Negro cook safe.

Andrew Weikert, Helena Party

Yellow Wolf's Account of the Helena Party Encounter:

"It was coming towards sundown when we saw a white man standing in the doorway of a house. We stopped not far from him but did not dismount. We sat on our horses, six or seven of us, thinking. *Chuslum Hahlap Kanoot* (Naked-footed Bull) said to me, 'My two brother and next younger brother were not warriors. They and a sister were killed at Big Hole. It was just like this man did that killing of my brother and sister. He is nothing but a killer to become a soldier sometime. We are going to kill him now. I am a man! I am going to shoot him! When I fire, you shoot after me.' Naked-footed Bull then fired and clipped his arm. As he made to run another warrior, *Yettahtapnat Alwum* (Shooting Thunder) shot him through the belly."

Works Consulted

Abbot, Karen. *Liar, Temptress, Soldier, Spy: Four Women Undercover in the Civil War* HarperCollins NY:NY © 2014

Beal, Merrill D. *"I Will Fight No More Forever."* University of Washington Press. Seattle:WA ©1963.

Benedict, Isabel. "The Killing of the Indian by Sam Benedict Denied, a True and Full Account of the Affair by Mrs. Benedict." Lewiston Teller, April 26, 1878. http://chroniclingamerica.loc.gov/lccn/sn82007023/1878-04-26/ed-1/seq-1/ Retrieved 4/9/2016

Chittenden, *"The Yellowstone National Park"* © 1895

Collins, Charles D., Jr. *Staff Ride Handbook and Atlas for the Battle of White Bird Canyon, 17 June 1877.* Combat Studies Institute Press. http://usacac.army.mil/CAC2/CSI/index.asp Retrieved 10/3/2016.

Jeffery, Julie Roy. Converting the West. A Biography of Narcissa Whitman. Norman and London. University of Oklahoma Press. © 1991.

Guie, H.D., McWhorter, Lucullus. *Adventures in Geyser Land.* The Caxton Printers, Ltd. Caldwell: ID © 1935.

Haines, Aubrey L. *Battle of Big Hole: The Story of the Landmark Battle of the 1877 Nez Perce War.* Globe Pequot Press. Helena: MT © 2007.

Howard, O.O. "My Life and Experiences among Our Hostile Indians." https://archive.org/stream/mylifeexperience00howa#page/254/mode/2up/search/Nez+Perce Retrieved 3/18/2017

https://archive.org/stream/yellowwolfhisown002070mbp/yellowwolfhisown002070mbp_djvu.txt Accessed 3/21/2016

https://history.idaho.gov/sites/default/files/uploads/Camas_%20Meadows_Camp_and_Battle_Sites_89001081.pdf

http://www.fs.usda.gov/detail/npnht/learningcenter/history-culture/?cid=fsbdev3_055745

http://missoulanews.bigskypress.com/missoula/a-yellowstone-tale/Content?oid=1674516

http://www.nps.gov/parkhistory/online_books/nepe/greene/chap2a.htm Accessed 3/21/2016

http://www.nps.gov/parkhistory/online_books//nepe/shs/chap13.htm Accessed 3/21/2016

http://www.ourheritage.net/index_page_stuff/following_trails/chief_joseph/chief_joseph_timeline.html Accessed 3/10/2016

http://theappendix.net/issues/2012/12/local-history-excerpt-i-rode-with-red-scout

http://www.yellowstonegate.com/2012/07/emma-cowan-captured-indians-yellowstone/?utm_source=rss&utm_medium=rss&utm_campaign=emma-cowan-captured-indians-yellowstone

http://www.idahogenealogy.com/bannock/nez_perce_indian_war_bannock_county.htm

McDermott, John D. *Forlorn Hope: The Nez Perce Victory at White Bird Canyon*. Caxton Press, University of Nebraska. © 1978.

McWhorter, L.V. *Hear Me, My Chiefs!"* The Canton Printers Ltd. Caldwell:ID © 1952.

Poe, J.W. "Beginning of the Nez Perce Hostilities." Lewiston Teller, April 13, 1878. http://chroniclingamerica.loc.gov/lccn/sn82007023/1878-04-13/ed-1/seq-2.pdf Retrieved 4/1/2016.

Schweber, Nate. "Local History Excerpt: I Rode With Red Scout: When Yellowstone's Early Tourists Stumbled into Chief Joseph and the Nez Perce's Final War." Feb 13, 2013. http://theappendix.net/issues/2012/12/local-history-excerpt-i-rode-with-red-scout

Scott, General Hugh L. U.S.A "Some Memories of a Soldier." N.Y.: London. © 1928.

Stanley, Edwin J. Rambles in Wonderland, or A Trip Through the Great Yellowstone Park. © 1898 5th Ed.

Stearns, Harold Joseph. A History of the Upper Musselshell Valley to 1920. University of Montana © 1966.

Topping, E.S. "Chronicle of Yellowstone." © 1888.

Weikert, Andrew J. "Journal of the Tour Through Yellowstone National Park, Vol III." Contributions to the Historical Society of Montana. © 1900.

End Notes

[i] Josiah Red Wolf, as he later became known, lived until March 23, 1971. He had been the first one to turn a shovel of dirt at the Nez Perce National Historical Park's visitor center in 1967.

[ii] Yellow Wolf recalled that after the battle the old man rode horseback from the camp. He recovered from the wounds and lived through the Nez Perce War, ending his life as a prisoner of War and dying where they were exiled to after surrendering. This was *Eeikish Pah* (Hot Place—the Nez Perce name for Indian Territory, present day Oklahoma)

[iii] Also another of the original 3 murderers, Red Moccasin Tops, died that morning.

[iv] Between 63 to 87 Nez Perce had been killed or mortally wounded, 30 or more of whom were women and children.

[v] Irwin's sojourn with the Nez Perces lasted six days until September 1, when he managed to escape. After escaping he was criticized for what he apparently told the Nez Perces about tourists in the park. "His sole motive in his talk and movements were to preserve his own life, which is a natural impulse." Bozeman *Times*, September 20, 1877.

"The first seen of him was late in the afternoon, about September 1, when Captain S.G. Fisher, Chief of Bannock Scouts, discovered him coming back on the trail. Fisher thought that he might be a renegade with the hostiles, so he covered him with his gun and challenged him. Irwin thought that Fisher was a renegade, on account of being with wild Indians (the Bannocks). They finally identified each other, and Irwin told us that while prisoner he acted as guide, and that Shively was boss packer for the squaw pack train and was watching his chance to *klatawa*. Shively was kept prisoner several days. He made a swift escape one night.

Irwin said that he supposed Fisher's scouts were connected with the hostiles, and that he was going to surrender and take chances on escaping again. He camped with the scouts that night, and the next day started down and back the main trail, reaching the command and telling General Howard about the awful stretch of down timber along Pelican Creek. He told General Howard that he could guide him down the river, over Mount Washburn to Baronett's Bridge, then up the East Fork of the Yellowstone and up to Soda Butte Creek, thus making a big cut-off to the headwaters of Clark's Fork. Although it involved some tough traveling across rough ravines and hell-roaring creeks that emptied into the main Yellowstone, it was certainly a cut-off of some seventy-five miles, or maybe more. And, after striking Soda Butte Creek, the traveling was very good indeed.

Irwin's information to General Howard certainly did save many miles of marching, by taking the short cut. He may have acted as guide from Mud geyser down to Baronett's Bridge, and probably did, but I don't remember seeing him after that. From the way he talked, I don't think that he tried to mislead the hostiles or tangle them up. He was taking them in general northerly direction, and that was the way they wanted to go, anyway, until they swung back to sort of a northwest course.

My impression is that Irwin was afoot when he met Fisher's scouts, although I may be mistaken about it. I know that Shively escaped afoot, for we followed the tracks of his big boots along a muddy creek bottom for half a mile, but never overhauled him."
-Colonel J.W. Redington as told to Frank Carpenter

[vi] See the Appendix for journal and Indian accounts of the Helena Party members' experiences.

[vii] Second Lieutenant Hugh L. Scott, guided by a local man, Collins J. ("Jack") Baronett found Dietrich's body still warm to the touch.

[viii] The warrior who treed Ben Stone was later interviewed by Duncan McDonald, a half-breed newspaper reporter who wrote an account of the war from the Indians' perspective.

The Indian was *We-ah-ton-nah-lah-Kah-wit* (Dawn-of-Day. He was a good representative of the Indians, stood 5 foot 9 inches tall and had aged between 23 and 25 years. McDonald was at a council in the Sioux camp when he asked why Dawn-of-Day chased Ben. Knowing that he was black and not a white man, their enemy, it made no sense to Duncan why the Indian wanted to kill him. Dawn-of-Day replied, "I had heard that a black man's hair was good for sick ear, and I wanted to get some of it."

[x] After 6 weeks, Weikert returned from Helena and retrieved both Kenck's and Deitrich's bodies. He only was able to bring the wagon and casket within 50 miles of Kenck's body. He went the rest of the way on horse and carried the body back on horseback. Then he took both back to Helena. "This was about as lonely a ride as I ever took. Two dead men in the wagon and I had to travel that way for over 200 miles…Dietrich was a particular friend of mine, and I kept good the promise I made him the last time I saw him in giving him a decent burial."

Made in the USA
Las Vegas, NV
19 May 2021